LEGALLY ZEN

Kyla —
Words can't express how grateful
I am to have met you — truly.
Thank you for being a friend
and a sister. You are a huge
part of my story and I wouldn't
have it any other way ♡.

xo Kat

Tyler -

Words can't express how grateful I am to have met you. Thank you for being a friend and a sister. You are a huge part of my story and I couldn't love it any other way ♥

Taylor x

LEGALLY ZEN

A Professional Skeptic's Path to Finding Inner Peace

KAT REILLY

E
***

To request permissions, contact the publisher at
jennifer@entouragemedia.ca.

Editing: Jennifer Goulden
Editing and Interior Design: Chris Arnold

ISBN (Paperback): 978-1-0689121-8-4
ISBN (e-Book): 978-1-0689121-9-1
First Edition Printed in Canada: October 2025
1 2 3 4 5 6 7 8 9 10

ENTOURAGE
...

Published by Entourage Media
entouragemedia.ca

*For my beautiful daughter—
my greatest teacher and my north star.*

GRATEFUL

I am grateful to each and every reader who chooses to spend this time reading my story. To give thanks, I have put together a fun little pack of *Zen Extras* that are free for you. Visit *legallyzen.ca* to collect.

— Kat

CONTENTS

CONTENTS

CONTENTS

I Did Not Want to Write This Book

I didn't think I'd ever admit to any of this, much less put it in print. I am someone who likes to keep her private life, well, private. My Instagram account? Set to private. Facebook? Private. I have a couple of IG accounts for creative pursuits, but you won't find my face or real name on them. If I've done it all properly, you will not find a single embarrassing photo of me anywhere on the internet.

I'm a lawyer, after all. Professionalism and propriety are my bread and butter. It simply wouldn't do to have photos of me being human or having fun (or, heaven forbid, looking silly) floating around in the public domain. In law school, they tell you, "Your reputation is everything. Once it's lost, it's gone for good." Ever the good student, I heeded that advice.

My path has largely been of the straight and narrow variety. Reading since age four. Straight-A student. Academics, athletics, and career-focused. Sprinkle in some international travel, some solid friendships, and a couple of (unsuccessful) long-term romantic relationships, and you've got a pretty good picture of how I lived life for most of my twenties and thirties.

It was a fairly one-dimensional existence in many ways. What you saw was what you got. Anything deeper was off the radar entirely. Lawyers (even Canadian lawyers like myself) didn't concern themselves with anything of the hippie-dippie, woo-woo variety, much less write books about the topic. No psychics, no chakras. I was certifiably woo-free. *Because, science.*

To most people, it looked like I was living a successful, glossy, lawyer lifestyle. In many ways, they weren't wrong. I was moving at a pretty good clip on the highway of life with the sunroof open, my Chanel sunglasses on, and my venti iced oat latte in the cup holder. With a lead foot and my sights set firmly on the destination, there wasn't much time to stop for scenery. The faster I hit my goals and milestones, the better.

I was leaning in hard to my law career—with the paycheck and bags under my eyes to prove it—until one day, it all came screeching to a halt (literally). That's when something—my body, the Universe, a wine-infused bike riding mishap during a trip with the girls—momentarily forced my foot off the gas and begged me to *slow the f down*. Like any self-respecting professional at the top of her game, my first thought was, "Hell no."

Work hard. Study hard. Prove yourself. Make money. Make partner. Travel the world. Buy a house. Land a man. Have 1.5 beautiful kids. This was the plan, my formula for success and fulfillment. Time off for a brain injury? *As if!* Kidney failure? *Pshh.* Existential crisis? *Not on my watch.*

This is the true story of what happened when my body sent warning signals for me to stop and begged me to pay attention before it was too late. It's about how, for lack of any other options, I found myself diving into an Elle Woods-style, Harvard-calibre education on spirituality and woo in search of relief. And I was doing so *without* losing my belief in logic, evidence, or conventional medicine.

Just as lawyers conduct much of their business under the shroud of confidentiality, I undertook my woo explorations from the safety of the proverbial closet. And by that, I mean I've largely kept this part of my life under wraps for fear that people would think that I had partaken in the Kool-Aid (or apple cider vinegar, as it were) and that I'd swapped my hard-earned law degree for a pack of tarot cards.

Lawyers don't go on meditation retreats. Lawyers don't do cacao ceremonies. Lawyers don't jump off waterfalls in Costa Rica. *Lawyers. Don't. Woo.* Right? Moreover, no one who considers themselves a "professional" does either. Judges, doctors, nurses, bankers, politicians, finance bros: *zero woo.*

Evidently, a lot of what this smart, logic-driven, badass lawyer thought she knew turned out to be wrong. It just took a life-altering health scare to realize it.

I feel as if I've discovered the cheat codes for living an exciting, vibrant life I love *and* found a community of people who've just been waiting to share all of this with me. The biggest surprise of all is that I already knew many of the kindred spirits within this woo community—I had met them in courtrooms, banks, health clinics, classrooms, and gyms. I just didn't know who they were at heart. Until now.

CHAPTER ONE
I Have Questions

I remember doing a science project in grade 5 called "Horoscopes: Fact or Fiction." I wanted to know if horoscopes were real or nonsense. I ran a basic experiment: I asked friends and family to read their horoscopes in the newspaper each day and assess their accuracy against their real lives, then report their findings to me. It was fun and interesting to hear their responses, and I probably learned more about their personal lives than a fifth grader should know. In the end, there was no grand conclusion, no breakthrough. The verdict was mixed, with the horoscopes getting it right some of the time and wrong some of the time. But I got to ask my questions, and I earned a good grade, so I was satisfied for the time being.

I have always asked questions and demanded answers about

anything and everything—life, love, work, health, happiness . . . I'm surprised my first word wasn't "why?" Over the years, some of my friends have begun to refer to me as Curious Kat. *Upon reflection, I should have steered well away from this nickname because didn't curiosity kill the cat?* It feels like I've been on a lifelong quest for knowledge, solutions, and answers. It made me the ideal student in school and now, a pretty damn good lawyer (if I do say so myself).

But asking certain questions can get you in trouble, particularly if they are of the hippie-dippie woo-woo variety. At some point, society decided that a belief in *something more* requires the distrust of nearly everything else. It was decided that people who are into "spiritual" things must be flaky, out of touch with reality, and unwilling or unable to participate in regular society.

I will confess that, for many years, I, too, relied on this kind of mental shorthand—especially when it concerned anything spiritual. I'd read about robe-wearing Buddhist Monks who all looked the same and devoted their lives to ancient texts and intense meditation—and it all sounded kind of culty to me.

I used to believe that people who woo'd (yep, I'm making it a verb) were very much *not* my people. As far as I was concerned, that crowd was made up of a bunch of hippie-dippie, pot-smoking idealists who didn't have real jobs, had taken a vow of poverty, and were living in communes with their fellow woo-woos.

Frankly, I was also pretty confident that being a lawyer who drives an SUV, never misses an episode of *The Bachelorette*, and wears power suits to court meant I was not *their* kind of person either—which was fine with me. I had my own life to focus on.

Lucky Number 7

I was on my way. The road ahead wasn't so much a road as a partnership track, and that track was paved with designer handbags and French-tip manicures. I had achieved many of the mile markers on my carefully plotted path to success: I had survived law school, been called to the bar, landed a job at one of the country's largest corporate law firms, was building my reputation as a young lawyer, and was making bank. It was finally time to buy a place of my own.

I loved the idea of owning my own home without having to depend on anyone else to share the mortgage. There was freedom in that. My mentality could be summed up by the lyrics to one of my life-long anthems, "Independent Women, Part 1," by Destiny's Child. I'm paraphrasing here, but the gist is: you see these shoes, these clothes, this bling, this house, this car? I bought it all because I am a grown-ass, independent woman. Both the poet and the fiercely independent woman in me will always be low-key obsessed with that song.

Twenty-nine-year-old me had been diligently saving up for a down payment since the second I paid off my student loans, and as I approached my thirtieth birthday, I realized I had enough money to put a down payment on a one-bedroom condo. The real estate market was pretty hot by the time I started condo shopping, and I had heard tons of stories from friends and acquaintances about the heartbreak they'd experienced putting offers in, being outbid in bidding wars, and losing out on places time after time.

After just three weeks of browsing, I was hitting a bunch of open houses one Saturday afternoon with my realtor, and I found the place. It was a condo on the top floor of a four-floor building. It had vaulted ceilings, skylights, and a cute little balcony that overlooked the interior courtyard, and it was in a lively, eclectic, up-and-coming neighbourhood. The climate of the housing market at the time was very much "you snooze, you lose." And I didn't like losing.

I had such a good feeling about the condo that I went back for a private viewing the following day, just to be sure. As soon as I set foot inside the space for the second time, I felt it again. I could envision myself living there, retreating to the balcony with a glass of wine after a long day, or having friends over on the weekend. This place was me. I loved it. And I wanted it. So I went all in. Or rather, my realtor, Alana, did.

Alana wasn't just my realtor; she was an old high school friend of mine and, like me, she was a hardworking, super keen go-getter. She so badly wanted to help me get this place that she went after it as if it were her own. I loved her for that.

By eight o'clock that Sunday evening, Alana was sitting across from me in my fifteenth-floor downtown office, writing up the offer and getting my signature on the various documents. We were told that the seller had intentionally priced the condo on the low side to elicit multiple bids. We knew full well that meant I would need to bid strategically if I were to have any hope of beating out the other bidders.

We settled on a dollar amount that was slightly above the asking price and also slightly above what we thought other people's slightly-above-asking-price bids would be.

"There's still a chance you won't get this property, Kat," she warned me, hoping to stave off any heartbreak I might have in the event I lost the bid.

"Yeah, I know. But I can totally see myself there. I really, really want this place, Alana!" It was shocking to see how quickly something I didn't know existed a day before could end up being so important to me by the end of the weekend.

Then Alana said something that caught me by surprise: "Okay! Now we pick a lucky number and put it in the offer! What's your lucky number?"

I laughed. "Seven is my number, but I don't think a number is going to save me here unless it's an added zero."

I'd watched enough episodes of *The Price is Right* in my childhood to know that an extra seven dollars, or even seven hundred dollars, wasn't going to make a difference in this kind of bidding war. It was simple: if someone outbid me, it would be by a larger margin than that. But I'd been a competitive athlete growing up, and there was always an element of superstition in sports that any serious competitor couldn't ignore. Some athletes had a lucky hat, some had lucky socks (ew), and now, as we wrote up this offer, I realized that

I needed to call my lucky number off the bench and see if she could help me work some magic.

My number was seven. It had always been seven. Partly because I was born on the 7th day of the month, and partly because my dad indoctrinated my sister and me into becoming New York Yankees fans growing up. We were a BIG baseball household and all of us wore #7 jerseys in honour of Mickey Mantle, the legendary Yankee. What can I say? Sports and superstition just go together.

"Okay—do it. Add a seven," I announced. Just saying it out loud made me feel like I had somehow improved my chances of getting the place (absurd, right?).

Alana amended the offer to include a seven and sent everything off to the seller's agent. They were accepting bids until 9 p.m., so it would be either later that night or the following morning before we found out if mine was the winning one.

"Sit tight, cross your fingers and toes, and we'll see what happens!" Alana said cheerfully and went home.

Eventually, I packed it in and went home, too. I was too distracted to work much longer. After getting home, I was doing my best to wind down—pyjamas on, cat on my lap, wine in hand, episode of *The Hills* cued up—when my phone rang. It was Alana.

"Oh, God!" I jumped, scared the shit out of Charlie the cat, and almost dumped red wine all over my pristine white sofa. "Shit!" I had to get it together. I put my glass down, picked up my phone, and hit the green answer button.

Instead of saying "Hello," like a normal person, I said, "I didn't get it, did I?" I was ready to cry. Badass-Lawyer-Kat persona be damned.

"No, no. Katherine!! You got it!!"

"Wait. What?" It took a moment to comprehend her words. My mind got stuck on the whole "no" part.

"You got the condo," she repeated slowly, making sure I understood what she was saying.

As it sank in, I screamed, "I just bought a fucking condo!" I must have blown out Alana's eardrums, but she didn't seem to notice.

"You bought a fucking condo!!" She confirmed, matching my energy, as I knew she would.

I hung up and happy-danced like a gleeful little weirdo around my apartment. I would be continuing to live the dream, but now I'd be doing it from the comfort of a home with my name on the deed.

I went to bed ecstatic, wired, stunned, and filled with new questions. Was this real? I only bid on one property, and I got it? In this market?? WTAF. When I finally got to sleep that night, I dreamt of the Yankees, my competitive softball days with my sister, and lucky number seven.

CHAPTER TWO
Warning Signs

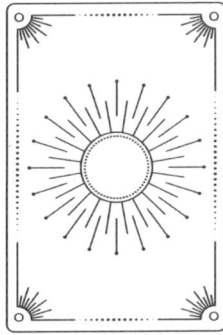

A fter my glorious victory in the Condo Bidding War of 2010, it felt like I was winning at both life and work. The young gun Lawyer Kat version of me was proudly working hard and playing hard. I enjoyed my singledom, my friends, and was working my buns off to learn anything and everything I could so that I could better kick ass at my job.

When I was at work, I had tunnel vision. I knew what I was doing and was dedicated to climbing my way to the top of the heap. But that didn't mean I didn't get some time to play, too.

On one Labour Day weekend, I went to a nearby wine region with friends for our annual bike-riding, wine-tasting camping trip. We called the yearly trip "Tastes Like Grape," based on our theory that people who said they could detect notes of leather, stone fruit, or honeysuckle in their wine were a bunch of wankers. I was wilfully blind to the mounting evidence that I was becoming a wanker myself. Drinking expensive wine was just something lawyers did. The ones I knew anyway.

The trail we were riding on was an old rail bed. I'm talking a 2 percent grade, which meant it was pretty much flat—except, that is, for the very short, rather gentle downhill section where the Universe tried to give me my first wake-up call.

There I was, pedalling through wine country along a picturesque path on a bike I had borrowed from a friend. As I was trundling down the only small hill on the entire route, I felt myself picking up a bit too much speed, so I applied the brakes. I've been told by my friends (my brain has mercifully spared me the precise memory of what followed) that the back brakes on the bike I was riding *didn't. fucking. work.* What the hell? They were working perfectly when we cruised on the safe, even terrain between wineries. Evidently, the deathly downhill portion of the trip was the best and most appropriate time for the brakes to take early retirement. Thanks a lot.

What happens when you slam on the brakes and only the front ones work, you ask? Well, if you're me, you unceremoniously fly ass-over-teakettle, hit your head on the ground, and land sprawled out on a dirt path, unconscious.

When I came to, one of my best girlfriends, Devin, was kneeling beside me, literally scooping gravel out of my mouth. She later told me that because of the contorted, scarecrow-esque fashion in which I had landed on the ground, she was worried I had broken my neck.

Devin was a nursing student at the time and—bless her heart—was one of those take-charge kind of friends who knew exactly what to do. She shooed away the rest of the group, made sure no one moved my body (in case I *had* broken my neck), and proceeded to gently remove the gravel from my mouth so that my airway wouldn't be impeded. Then she and another friend took me to the nearest hospital.

I was examined by the ER doctor and told I had a concussion. I remember being annoyed because working hard and playing hard didn't leave time for frivolous activities such as concussion recovery time.

That night, my friends (I am so lucky to have friends like these) set alarms for themselves throughout the night and took turns coming to wake me up every two hours to make sure I didn't fall into a coma—or whatever the reason is that someone with a fresh concussion isn't supposed to sleep for more than two hours at a time.

I went straight back to work the following Monday because, as a third-year lawyer who was intent on proving herself and her worth, I wasn't about to stop for a bump on the head. I got back on the proverbial horse and headed to work like nothing happened.

Within a week or two, I realized that a strange fogginess had settled over me. I just didn't feel like myself. (I later learned that this is an incredibly common feeling among concussion sufferers.)

It was annoying and a bit scary, but I pushed on. I had things to do, people to cross-examine, and cases to win.

"Not feeling like myself" struck me as a pretty weak kind of complaint and, in my concussed (but still proud) mind, it wasn't nearly enough to warrant taking time off work.

The pace at work was relentless. There were weeks when I wrote hundred-page-long legal briefs and nights when I only slept three or four hours. I kept my feet moving, one in front of the other. Luckily for me, I loved my job and took comfort in knowing exactly what my future looked like.

Before I realized it, a year had passed by. My symptoms persisted. I worked through a haze, as if I were floating at times. Things that used to come easily to me took way more effort and concentration than they used to. Things like decision-making, thinking fast, and even moving my body at a regular pace demanded Herculean levels of energy.

Sometimes my morning routine dragged on for a painfully long time, and I felt like I just couldn't get myself out of the house. I later learned that time management, organization, and other "executive functioning" tasks felt harder because of the concussion. I soldiered on, but I hated that everything felt exponentially more difficult than it should.

A friend of a friend heard me complaining about the lingering fogginess one day over brunch and convinced me to see someone. This person happened to be in the medical profession, and she connected me to a neurologist that she worked with. On the strength of her direct referral, I skipped the queue, which in Canada saved me months of waiting. I got in to see Dr. Bradley, an older, extremely kind neurologist who was known to be one of the best in his field. I described my symptoms and waited while he went through the usual suite of tests to determine whether I was crazy or if I had an actual problem.

Turns out, it was neither.

"Overall, your brain seems fine," he said. "It is just taking some time to recover."

Um . . . *Some* time? "But it's already been a year," I said, exasperated. "I need my brain in working order to do my job."

Dr. Bradley empathized but didn't have any more answers for me, at least not the ones I wanted. I just needed to "give it some more time." I was trying to comprehend how on earth I could continue to survive twelve-hour work days and be a badass lawyer under this semi-permanent gauzy haze. I could work without a lot of things, but my brain was not one of them. Losing a limb would have been easier, I thought to myself.

I walked out of Dr. Bradley's office, left the hospital grounds, and waited for a bus to take me back downtown to my office. I sat on that bus, crying silent tears, and tried not to look out the window (the passing streets and scenes sometimes made me dizzy). Brain fog, the amorphous feeling of being out of my body, the fight to just do my job, the lack of energy, the inability to get a decent night's sleep . . .

How much longer would "some time" be? Did that mean this was just my life now?

When I got back to work, I stopped in the bathroom, dried my tears, fixed my makeup, and went back to my desk.

It felt like life or the Universe or *something* was telling me to slow down, but I didn't have time to listen.

I had shit to do. Things at work were full steam ahead. Besides, this lady now had mortgage payments to make. It would take more than a winery tour injury to take me down. Time passed, and slowly but steadily things began to improve.

Lesson Learned (Sort Of)

I didn't know it yet, but there's a saying in the spiritual community that the Universe keeps giving you the same lesson until you finally learn it. Well, it turned out I wasn't the top student I thought I was, because I wasn't truly learning from any of the lessons the Universe was throwing at me.

The Universe dealt me a second (stern) warning a few months later, on an evening I'll never forget.

As my path to success dictated, I'd been focusing on advancing my career, making money, becoming partner, buying a home, and eventually, landing a man and having kids (looking back, I'm not sure if I was truly living life as a human *being* or just a human *doing*). But to eventually land said man and have said kids, I would need to date someone first.

Boyfriends were few and far between for me, and I hadn't dated anyone seriously since my law school relationship had ended a few years earlier. Love was on my list of must-haves, but unlike school or work, a loving, committed relationship wasn't the kind of thing I could generate simply by putting in enough effort, which made the whole endeavour pretty frustrating.

To top it off, trying to shoehorn personal time into my schedule was kind of like playing Tetris. If I could find a way to fit something in, I would. Otherwise, my work tasks piled up on each other, and before I knew it, it was game over.

One particular weeknight, the stars had aligned (or so I thought), and I'd managed to schedule a date with someone I'd met online. I stayed at the office for as long as I could before taking a cab directly to the restaurant to meet up with the guy—let's call him Chad.

Chad was nice enough, but I could tell from the jump that he was *not* the guy for me. This was going to be a one-drink-then-home-to-bed kind of evening.

I had my glass of wine, he had ginger ale, we engaged in some banal chitchat, and then I explained that I had a long day at work the next day and needed to get going.

I fully intended to take a cab home, but Chad, who, to be fair, seemed like a genuinely nice guy, offered to drive me. I could tell he was also angling for a second date. I went back and forth about whether to let this stranger see what building I lived in. Chad, sensing my reluctance, reassured me, "Look, I'm just gonna drive you home and drop you off; the worst thing that'll happen is you'll see what a shitty car I drive."

Oh, Chad, if only that had been true.

Chad radiated harmless puppy dog vibes, making it hard to say no. He seemed earnest and just wanted to do something gentlemanly for me, so I accepted the ride, and he walked me to his car. He wasn't lying; it was an old beater. I got in and gave him directions to my condo.

We were headed toward my place, and a few blocks ahead of time, I told Chad what street to turn onto next. He was looking intently at street signs, not wanting to miss the turn. But, in looking a block or two ahead for street signs, he was looking *past* the traffic light that was directly in front of and above us.

The whole thing unfolded in slow motion (for me). We were approaching a red light, but Chad wasn't braking. I started yelling for Chad to slow down, but by the time he realized what was happening and hit the brakes, it was too late. We had run the red light and T-boned a massive SUV that had been going along on its merry way, driving through a green light.

The front of Chad's crappy little car was pretty crunched up, but we both got out and appeared to be unharmed. I must have been stunned because I didn't ask for anyone's names or contact information. I didn't take any pictures. I didn't wait for the police to come. I literally just stood on the curb, hailed a cab, and went home to bed.

True to form, I was like, *fuck this shit—I have work in the morning. I'm outta here.*

Chad texted me the next day to see how I was. He broached the topic of a second date but said he'd understand if I didn't want to see him again—you know, given the whole car crash thing. I wasn't sure whether it was kinder to tell him that he was never in the running for a second date to begin with or to let him think that it was because of the car accident, but I declined the offer and never saw him again.

After the car accident date with Chad, I figured, at the very least, I'd always have the winning answer anytime people were comparing stories about "worst first dates ever." Little did I know that incident would kick off one of the most meaningful, life-changing chapters of my story.

Brain Fog

About three days after the crash, I knew something was wrong. My brain had become foggy, achy, and slower than molasses in a way I had not previously felt. I dragged myself across the street to a walk-in clinic and saw a doctor, who matter-of-factly informed me that brain swelling from a concussion doesn't always show up right away. It typically takes three to five days for your brain to swell. Sneaky bugger.

If my symptoms persisted or worsened, the doctor suggested I follow up with my family doctor to see about getting further treatment. I went back to work and tried to forge ahead despite how awful I was feeling. Things did not improve, and, eventually, I made an appointment with my family doctor, Dr. Leigh.

It took more than one appointment with Dr. Leigh for her to appreciate the magnitude of what I was dealing with. At one point during an appointment, she patted my knee (literally) and said, "You're just feeling this stuff intensely because you're used to functioning at such a high level!"

I really could have done without the slightly patronizing ego boost; I just needed my concerns to be listened to. Looking back, I think Dr. Leigh's reaction inadvertently reinforced my mindset that I should just tough it out and try not to let this injury stop me from doing all my normal activities. However, even I couldn't ignore how crappy I felt. Things were most definitely getting worse, not better.

So, back I went to the doctor.

Once my complaints stopped being dismissed and minimized, I managed to get a referral to a neuropsychologist, Dr. Cheryl Rose.

*A **neuropsychologist** is a psychologist who specializes in testing and diagnosing brain disorders. They come up with treatment plans for conditions like brain injuries, including concussions like mine, and other disorders.*

Dr. Rose was a classy, elegant Jewish woman who had moved to Canada from New York. Her suits were beautifully tailored but still understated. She was soft-spoken, highly educated, and successful.

I had an instant girl crush. She was ten or fifteen years older than I was, and she had five kids. *Five kids?!* This woman was clearly a superhero. Also, I was in a pretty desperate place, and I wanted more than anything for her to be the answer to my prayers.

Dr. Rose was stunned that it took nearly six months for me to make my way to her through the Canadian healthcare system. And her jaw actually dropped when I admitted to taking a taxi home from the car wreck without asking for anyone's contact info or waiting for the police. "Obviously, you were in shock," she said. Thinking back, I realized how absurd it was that I'd behaved that way. "Huh. Yeah, I guess I was," I replied. "I hadn't thought about it like that before."

Dr. Rose informed me that the fact that we were six months post-concussion meant we were in a whole different ballpark in terms of medical recommendations and protocols. Hiding out in a dark room for a week wasn't going to save me at this point. *Fantastic.*

My symptoms not only persisted, but they got noticeably worse. The fog was thicker, denser. I was dizzy, off-balance, and disoriented. I remember telling a friend, "I'm worried people are going to think I'm drunk in the middle of the day because sometimes I lose my balance just walking down the sidewalk." Conversations felt distant, like I was floating above them. At work, I felt like a space alien in heels. Words slipped away as I reached for them. Lights hurt my head, and things sometimes went blurry without warning. Headlights were hell, so I hated driving at night.

Under the care of Dr. Rose, I received bi-weekly counselling sessions (having a therapist who also knows the ins and outs of brain injuries was an absolute game changer), plus I was seeing any other specialist or practitioner whom she thought I should see. She was essentially quarterbacking my treatment plan. Even though I didn't feel better yet, I loved having someone on my team who was as invested in my recovery as I was.

Stay in the Game

Meanwhile, on a day-to-day basis, I did my best to ignore every sign my body sent me and pushed ahead. I tried to focus on living a "normal" life, which for me meant working sixty-plus-hour weeks and fitting in multiple medical appointments each week, then crying into my margarita(s) on my day off.

Adding insult to injury, I ended up in a lawsuit of my own. The accident had changed everything, but the insurance company wasn't about to help me without a fight first. And so the medical bills kept piling up. (Canadian health care only stretches so far.)

I told myself that being a lawyer would make the lawsuit easier. *Big bad insurance company v. badass lawyer? No sweat!* I thought I'd know how to handle it. But I was wrong. The whole thing was low-key traumatic. I sat under oath and was cross-examined. I spent hours in sterile offices while doctors poked, prodded, and wrote reports, passing judgment on whether my pain was "serious enough."

Daily life had me looking over my shoulder. If I lifted a grocery bag or went for a walk, I worried that someone was watching—an investigator, camera in hand—waiting for some magic proof that I wasn't really sick, that I didn't really need help.

One night in particular, I was sitting in my office in the high-rise building downtown where my firm was located. Lawyers tend to work late (some of what you see in the TV shows is true to form), but that night I was working later than most. I was the only person left on my floor. I was in the middle of a gruelling trial and working on witness prep that needed to be done for the next day.

I was battling a migraine (my new normal). Concussion number two came with the bonus gift of chronic migraines—in the clinical sense, this meant I had migraines for more than half the days of every month. I would have a brutal headache for two, three, sometimes five days at a time. Then I'd get a couple of days' reprieve before I was plunged back into another painful migraine. These migraines weren't *fully* debilitating, like some others I've experienced, but they meant I was living in a loud, harsh, foggy place most of the time.

There I was, sitting at my desk, struggling to concentrate, distracted, and intensely frustrated by the construction noise coming from the floor above me. My head was pounding, and my work was taking *forever* because my productivity was at an all-time low. I couldn't concentrate and kept getting distracted by every little thing. The witness prep that I thought would take an hour, hour and a half tops, was dragging on for four, then five hours. I had gut rot from all the coffee I'd had that day. I hadn't eaten dinner because I was trying to push through and finish my work before taking a dinner break.

MANTRA #1:

Play like it doesn't hurt.

I wasn't listening to what my body was telling me. I learned during my competitive fast-pitch softball days that the better course of action was to "play like it didn't hurt."

The theory was that, if you were injured but wanted to keep playing (which I always did), you needed to play like it didn't hurt—because if you played like you *were* hurt, you would sub-consciously favour the hurt body part or shy away from the ball, trying to protect the injured area. Worst case scenario number one: you might injure yourself even worse because you weren't using the skills and techniques that you had spent countless hours learning and practising. Worst-case scenario number two: you would flub the play because you were preoccupied with the injury instead of focused on the ball. I learned this strategy early on in my softball career.

I don't want to throw any of my beloved coaches under the bus. They were caring, dedicated people who were passionate about the sport, and if I was hurt, none of them were forcing me to stay in the game. Without fail, *I* was forcing myself to stay in the game. *I* wanted to win. *I* wanted to play. I did *not* want to sit on the sidelines. Mind you, I didn't get a lot of pushback when I said I wanted to keep playing. I was a strong player, and I helped my team win games. So when I played hurt, everyone was happy.

Except for my poor body, that is. My body most definitely "kept the score."[1]

I finally finished my witness prep sometime after 11 p.m. I went home and had a big fat glass of wine to help me relax (a "generous" pour, as I liked to call it). I melted into the couch for an hour, then washed the day off and crawled into bed. Eventually, I drifted off, and six or seven hours later, my alarm went off and I did some version of it all over again. I was doing a horrible job of paying attention to the mounting evidence that pointed directly toward the demise of my health.

Thanks, Universe

I tried to make sure I still had a life outside of just home, court, and the office. It was my friend Rosie's birthday, and a bunch of us spent the day with her, taking her around town doing things she loved. It was a much-needed distraction from pain and symptoms for me.

First, we went for foot massages and then stopped for pie and coffee at this tiny, local, legendary pie spot. In those days, you hadn't had pie until you'd had pie at Aphrodite's.

The only open parking spot on the street was in front of the metaphysical store, so when we went back to the car, one of the girls, Joey, suggested we go in and check out the oracle decks.

_____

1 Van der Kolk, Bessel A., _The Body Keeps the Score: Brain, Mind, and Body in the Healing of Trauma_ (Penguin Books, 2015).

Her aunt was into that sort of thing, making her the automatic group expert.

Back in the day, the word *metaphysical* wasn't even in my vocabulary, so I wouldn't have called it that. I just thought of it as a hippie bookstore full of crystals, tarot cards, and other nonsense.

We went into the store (which reeked of incense) and browsed around for a bit before making our way over to the wall of oracle decks, which looked a lot like tarot cards to me.

"They're different from tarot, but I'm not exactly sure how," Joey explained. Her aunt had a bunch of oracle decks, and the way she had done it was to pick a deck, shuffle the cards, and then choose one card and read what the accompanying guidebook had to say about it.

"Ooooh! A Spirit Animal deck!" gasped Joey and pulled one of the decks from the shelf.

"Oh God, this should be good," I laughed, rolling my eyes.

Joey wasn't phased. She was in her element.

The girls drew their cards one by one, and then it was my turn. I picked mine but didn't look at it right away. It felt like the kind of moment you make a wish. I was the only one in the group who was still single, and I had been struggling with all of this health stuff, so I quietly hoped for something bold, something majestic, like a phoenix or an eagle. When I finally flipped over my card, we all looked down at it and burst out laughing.

It may not have been a *warning* sign, but it was most

definitely *a* sign. It was a cougar. The single thirty-something woman pulled a cougar.

Ha ha. Very funny. Thanks, Universe.

CHAPTER THREE
Desperate Meditation

I t had been about two years since the accident, and I *still* had symptoms without any signs of letting up. *Un-effing-believable. I object!*

Determined not to be branded as the "brain-injured lawyer", I had kept my second concussion a secret from all but two of my close work friends. I didn't want people questioning my ability or capacity, nor did I want their sympathy. I most certainly didn't want the plum files to go to another associate instead of me because people may have perceived me as injured in any way. So I kept my struggles private.

A mentor at work, Karla, recommended a couple of books to me while we were talking over lunch one day. I admired Karla. She loved life, kicked ass at her job, had three kids . . . She was doing it all and killing it! If Karla was recommending something, I was going to take that recommendation seriously. I had learned to listen to people who had made it to where I wanted to be in life.

The books Karla recommended were classified as spiritual books when I looked them up online. There were two titles in particular that Karla wanted me to read: *The Power of Now* by Eckhart Tolle and *The Untethered Soul* by Michael Singer. Karla had described to me how she had used these books as tools. They helped her learn to stay in the moment so that she could be fully present at work (even if she missed her kids or was veering into the land of "mom guilt"), and they helped her stay fully present when she was at home with her family—even if her phone was blowing up and clients were trying to get ahold of her at an unreasonable hour.

I took Karla's advice and bought both of the books. It felt weird to be reading *for me*, instead of reading case law or doing document review for one of my files at work. But, at the same time, I was sort of reading for work. More than ever, and unbeknownst to Karla, I wanted to stay sharp and be at the top of my professional game.

Those two books stirred something in me. I didn't realize it at the time, but a seed had been planted. It would just need a few more years for it to take root.

SOS

I wasn't getting better, but it wasn't for lack of trying. I had x-rays, blood tests, and even an MRI, which showed a lesion on my brain, likely from when I had hit the ground the first time. I also saw a myriad of therapists and specialists, many of whom I had been referred to by Dr. Rose. Rosie and I had begun to call Dr. Rose "the Swami" because her advice was always so on-point and she seemed so dialled in.

One of the experts I saw for treatment was a neurological physio-therapist named Paula. Dr. Rose had worked closely with Paula and highly recommended her. As I learned, neuro-physios focus on the treatment and rehabilitation of neurological conditions affecting the brain, spinal cord, and nerves. Yes, you read that right, my *brain* needed *physiotherapy*. I couldn't believe this was my life.

Thankfully, Paula was a gentle woman with a vast amount of expertise and a quiet confidence about her. I knew I was in good hands. In our sessions, we worked through some intense exercises intended to (eventually) ease my symptoms, but Paula warned: "With brain injuries like this, the road to recovery can be longer than you want, but recovery is possible."

I remember freezing. Did I hear her right? Since when did a full recovery become debatable? Paula was so sweet and caring that I found myself letting it all out in our sessions. I explained in excruci ating detail all the symptoms I'd been desperately trying to hide from the rest of the world. I told her how frustrated I was by how long it was taking to get back to some semblance of normalcy. Just feeling comfortable enough to be completely raw and vulnerable with her for a few moments was itself good medicine.

"I want you to go home and try a guided meditation," Paula said, once I had collected myself and dried my tears. She recommended starting with a body-scan meditation within a specific app.

I was sure she could see my "Yeah, right!" face. It sounded like hippie woo stuff. If other people wanted to practise meditation, as far as I was concerned, they could fill their boots, but I was addressing actual medical problems and needed real solutions.

As if reading my mind, she said, "There's more and more science behind the benefits of meditation. And it can't hurt to try, right?!"

I was growing increasingly desperate, so I accepted my homework assignment and downloaded the app. I think I did it the night before my next appointment. (Look, I said I was a good student; I never said I wasn't also a classic procrastinator.)

The thought of a silent-sitting-style meditation can be intimidating for anyone, especially if you're new to meditating. I'd tried once with a friend and lasted all of three minutes before I aborted the mission. I didn't want to be alone with my thoughts—or in silence, for that matter—forced to sit with things I usually preferred to drown out with noise or distraction. (Wasn't that what podcasts were for?) And the idea that I had to "empty" my mind or sit in complete stillness? Honestly, the whole thing just sounded (a) boring, and (b) impossible, especially since my brain was usually running in ten directions at once. I couldn't even imagine how difficult and daunting it might feel for someone who struggles with ADHD.

As a classic "all or nothing", "go big or go home" type of thinker, doing a guided meditation instead of a "real" meditation (whatever *that* is) felt like I was somehow cheating. Did it count if I needed to have a voice walk me through the process? I realize now how faulty these early assumptions were. I can assure you—it's not cheating at all. Guided meditations are perhaps the best possible way to ease into the world of meditation, and I would recommend this approach to anyone hesitant or intimidated but still curious about trying meditation.

The night before my next appointment with Paula, I sat down after work, poured myself a glass of wine, and found the meditation she had recommended. It was only eight minutes long. *Eight minutes . . . that's not so bad. Let's just get this over with*, I thought. I wanted to get my check mark at the next session so we could move on to something that actually worked.

I pressed play on the track and closed my eyes. The female voice implored me to "go on a journey through my body, in my mind, just seeing what's there."

Journey, my ass.

The voice ignored my thoughts and instructed me to focus on my forehead, now my ears . . . now my jaw . . . now my neck.

Oh, come on.

"Notice the sensations," she said. "Notice what's there."

Pain. Pain is there.

The voice continued, "Just notice what you're feeling . . . There's no need to judge or try to change anything."

Stop reading my mind, lady. Of course, I'm judging. Of course, I want to change how this feels.

I did make it through the full eight minutes, and like the wildly sarcastic, thoroughly annoyed, but still excellent student that I was, I decided to learn everything I could about meditation, Elle Woods-style. There are quite literally thousands of books and apps out there on mindfulness and meditation.

I found articles about the growing science behind meditation. To begin with, meditation is known to improve the quality of sleep and even help with falling asleep in the first place. It can also reduce stress and inflammatory response in the body, improve memory, improve attention span, reduce symptoms of anxiety and depression, reduce high blood pressure, and improve energy levels. And that was just the short list.

I appreciated that I could practise meditation anywhere, so I did it at home behind closed doors.

I read somewhere that most of us live in our heads most of the time (*check*), and some of us only live in our heads (*double check*). This can leave us feeling super disconnected from our physical body. So, if one were to, say, wipe out on a winery tour and avoid seeking medical help, and then, say, get in a car crash and suffer a second traumatic brain injury but refuse to take time off and instead tough it out, one could say—theoretically—that they had become an expert at disconnecting from their body and living exclusively in their head. (Um. *Triple-check*.)

I wasn't fully sold on meditation practice yet, but it was now a part of what my expert neuro-physiotherapist was recommending, so I persisted for the next couple of weeks, listening to the body scan at bedtime each night.

Turns out, meditation gets easier with practice. Hence, the reason it's called a practice. You're not supposed to be good at it from the get-go, and no matter how long you've been doing it, there is always something new to learn or observe. The idea is that, over time, it becomes easier to "drop in" (aka: the feeling of arriving into a deeply relaxed, meditative state).

As time went on, the body scan track would often lull me to sleep. Because I was struggling with a post-concussive sleep disorder, this was not a bad thing (although, I convinced myself that falling asleep partway through meant I was meditating "wrong"). As the meditation became more familiar, I settled into it more. And I did get better at *noticing* what was going on in my body. It took me a long time, however, to stop *judging* what I was noticing about what was going on in my body.

Doing the nightly body scan and relaxing my body into sleep meant that, bit by bit, I started getting more (and better quality) sleep at night, which meant having a bit more energy during the day. It was a small win, but it was a win.

I graduated beyond body scan meditation and tried other guided—and eventually non-guided—meditations. All the while, I struggled with perfectionism while meditating. There was often (i.e., *always*) a voice in my head telling me I wasn't doing it right if my mind wandered, if I missed a few days, or if I didn't have some cosmic breakthrough during a session. I was scared of what might come up—big, messy emotions I didn't want to face, let alone make space for. It was also hard to turn off the insistent voice telling me I didn't have time to meditate. But I *did* have time because *any* amount of time was enough. Five minutes. Ten. An hour. There are no rules.

Contrary to popular belief, your brain doesn't become empty when you're meditating properly, nor is that the point. The point is to notice where your mind is going when it wanders. Notice the thoughts and voices that are coming up. Acknowledge them and listen to what they are trying to tell you. Then, firmly but gently, usher them out the door, and bring yourself back into meditation. It's helpful to focus on your breath (especially if you're doing a silent sitting) or simply tune back into the words of the guided meditation.

Another hot tip that I wish I'd known when I started meditating: there's no such thing as a bad meditation. Meaning: whatever happens during my meditation, wherever my mind wanders to, I let it. It is all good information. Maybe it's a little prompt for me to take more breaks or move my body to help calm down my monkey mind. *(I think of the term "monkey mind" as a reference to when a person's mind is constantly jumping from thought to thought, making it hard to concentrate and stay focused. It's the chitter chatter that seems to fill your brain when you are trying to focus on stillness.)* Maybe it's letting you know that it's okay to be bothered by that thing your co-worker said—and it's okay to let it go now and not let it bother you anymore.

If you're meditation curious, maybe this will help . . .

Kat's Meditation Tips for Beginners

Meditation, or even just getting quiet with yourself (sometimes also referred to as a silent sitting), is as close to a gateway drug for woo as it gets, second only to yoga. Meditation is one of the most foundational tools that people can use (and have been using for centuries) to turn off the noise, become more centred, learn to turn inward, and find more about who they are inside.

Here's what I did to get started. Feel free to try it.

★ Start with shorter sessions (5 or 10 minutes, max).

★ Start with guided meditations if sitting silently with your thoughts is your definition of a living hell.

★ Remember that a clear or blank mind isn't the goal.

★ Your mind is going to wander (it's not if, it's when), and when it does, it's about observing, noting, and gently bringing yourself back.

★ Don't make it hard on yourself. Find a quiet space, a comfortable spot to sit, and turn off your phone notifications.

★ There is no such thing as a bad meditation; even a meditation where your monkey mind is going non-stop does not mean it was unsuccessful; it means you got some good information. Noticing that you were easily distracted is the key . . . and then maybe digging down from there to figure out why.

★ Try to go in with no expectations of what will come up for you during the meditation—try being the operative word.

★ Try to meditate regularly. Life happens, and there's no award for never missing a day. The real flex is getting back on the horse (or mat, as it were).

More Meditation

I have tried many kinds of meditation since those early days, and consider myself to be a semi-regular meditator. It's surprising how many ways there are to practise meditation. Here are some of the ways I've tried:

Mindfulness Meditation: This is what people often think of when they think of meditation. Mindfulness meditation has gained a lot of popularity these days, and with good reason. It is all about bringing you back to the present moment and maintaining awareness of your thoughts, feelings, and bodily sensations, without judgment. You can do mindfulness meditation in a more formal way, where you sit for a specific length of time, OR you can also incorporate mindfulness practices into your regular **day-to-day tasks!** Mindful walks, mindful eating, and mindfully brushing your teeth—these can all be meditative activities that bring you back into the present moment and into your body.

Body Scan Meditation: This was a great entry point for me because I had physical injuries. It involves paying attention to each part of the body in sequence, noticing physical sensations, and just noting what is there, without judgment of how it feels or if there is tension or pain.

Guided Meditation: Guided meditations can take many forms and typically involve following the guidance of a teacher's voice, whether live or recorded. The teacher will lead you through a specific meditation practice, such as visualization or body scan.

Yoga Nidra (aka lie down and chill out) is one of my favourite types of guided, body awareness meditation; the aim is to draw the attention inward and relax the body and mind so that you can find a state of equilibrium between wakefulness and sleep. Many people use yoga nidra to help them if they are having trouble sleeping. (If you want to say you're doing meditation and sound fancy, just lie down, close your eyes, and call it yoga nidra.)

Loving-Kindness (aka: Metta) Meditation: Metta meditation focuses on cultivating feelings of love, compassion, and goodwill towards oneself and others, sometimes through the repetition of positive affirmations. Yeah, right. I know what you're thinking. Send love to that a$$hole opposing counsel who wrote me that nasty letter yesterday? Um, no. Send love to the careless driver who cut me off in traffic? Sure. I'll try . . .

Breath Awareness Meditation: Pretty self-explanatory. Breath awareness meditation is focused on observing the rhythms and sensations of one's breath to anchor the mind in the present moment. Shout out to "Yoga With Adrienne" on YouTube and her at-home breath awareness mantra that I still use to this day.

Mantra Meditation: The repetition of a single phrase or sound can be a way to focus the mind during meditation. You can use a personal affirmation. My go-tos are "My breath is my anchor, my anchor is my breath" (again, *thank you Adrienne!*), or "this moment is exactly right" (when I want to remind myself that I trust in the larger plan and unfolding of what the Universe has in store for me). Some people prefer mantras like "I am safe, or "I am loved." Option B is to go with a mantra from one of the ancient spiritual traditions, like "*Om shanti*" or "*So hum.*"

Active or moving meditation: Yoga, Tai Chi, and Qi Gong are all considered to be forms of moving meditation. They're all slightly different, but they are three of the most popular mind-body exercises. Out of these, I have only practised Yoga, although I aspire to Tai Chi.

Somatics, while not a meditation style per se, is considered to be a field within bodywork and movement therapies studies that emphasizes full body awareness and focuses more on feeling the body and listening to the body, as opposed to mindlessly doing laps or reps of something in order to attain an exercise goal. Yoga, Tai Chi, and Qi Gong practices are all considered somatic practices. Search on YouTube for "somatic practices" and you will discover dozens more.

Mayo Clinic says, "Somatic practices recognize the interconnectedness of the physical body and mental/emotional states, and they use this connection to facilitate healing and personal growth."

Sound Meditation: Involves focusing on repetitive sounds and healing frequencies, such as chanting, singing bowls, or nature sounds, to induce a meditative state. There are some amazing (free) meditation apps available now, and tons of tracks available depending on what kind of soundscape you're in the mood for.

There are other meditation styles I haven't tried, such as **Transcendental Meditation** (sometimes referred to as **"TM"**) and **Zen Meditation**. Celebrities have been known to gravitate to TM, maybe because of the exclusivity surrounding it. Personally, this one feels a bit "shi-shi" and exclusionary to me, but I honestly haven't tried it.

Zen Meditation (aka: Zazen) is another meditation type, practised by the Zen Buddhist community. Unlike guided or mantra-based meditation, Zazen emphasizes simplicity—sitting in stillness, focusing on posture and breath, and observing thoughts without attachment. It is intended to help find clarity, presence, and awareness of the moment.

Somatics (and Semantics!) *Soma is Greek for body, so somatic simply means "of the body, or relating to the body." Anything and everything to do with the body is arguably somatic. Which is why it is redundant to speak of somatic yoga or suggest that it's a distinct type of yoga practice, because, well, all yoga is somatic. Anyhoo, we needn't get hung up on the semantics of somatics, but the word nerd in me just couldn't resist.*

CHAPTER FOUR
DIVINE TIMING

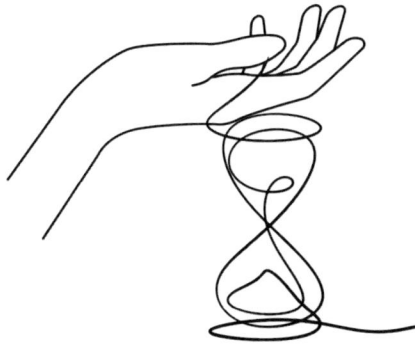

I am an impatient person (shocker, I know). If I want something, I want it now (or, preferably, yesterday). During this point in my journey, I was feeling particularly impatient—to be healed, to feel better, to get back to "normal." I didn't want to wait. I didn't want to slow down. I didn't want, well, any of it. I was pissed. But I was trying.

After getting the book and meditation prescriptions from my doctors and my mentor, I started to give this stuff a chance, and have since read a number of other spiritual books. Michael Singer has a book called *Living Untethered* in which he writes about divine timing. He describes how many millions of minute things and intricate occurrences had to fall into place in a particular way for us to encounter the moments we are encountering and to have the experiences we're having. This concept resonated with me.

We've all been there. We lost the car keys in the ocean while on vacation in Hawaii (*I swear, I safety-pinned them to my swimsuit and they seemed secure*), derailing our plans for the day and leaving us waiting for hours while a new set of keys, which cost hundreds of dollars to replace, is brought to us. *Not you? Just me? Fine.*

Anyhow, you end up driving back to your hotel only to find you missed a tragic car accident so bad that it closed down the entire freeway, and that it occurred right around when you would've been there hours prior.

Your friend cheerily announces from the backseat: "Guys, losing the keys was the best thing that could have happened to us! We spent the afternoon at the beach, but we could have just as easily been stuck on the freeway this whole time, waiting for it to reopen. Or, worse . . . we could have been one of the cars involved in the accident." The rest of us pause, taking this in. I raise my eyebrow but hold my tongue (for once) and keep on driving.

"Perhaps we *were* meant to lose the key," one of my other friends says. *Hmm. Doubtful, but worth considering*, I begrudgingly admit to myself.

Divine timing is similar to, *but has some important distinctions from*, the viewpoint that everything happens for a reason. Not everyone loves that idea.

"So why bother doing anything if whatever's going to happen

is going to happen?!" Someone who might sound and look like me sneers. "It's just a cop-out. A fatalistic excuse to throw our hands up in the air and stop trying."

But then I stop and think about the path and patterns of my life. There have been far too many events in my life that could have led to total disaster (or that I genuinely thought *were* leading to total disaster), but instead, led to outcomes better than I could have ever dreamed. If thousands of things had fallen into a slightly different order, my whole life would be different. *I* would be different. And, as you will come to learn, my life and I are pretty amazing now.

I like the idea that divine timing implies a larger plan is in place—that people, things, and events are interconnected in ways I often can't see or understand in the moment.

This concept is at the core of what spirituality means for so many of us—the belief in something larger than ourselves, something *outside* of us. I find comfort in the idea that everything happens in its own time, and because things will unfold exactly as they are meant to, there is no need to rush, no need to control the uncontrollable. As a recovering perfectionist, this concept gives me permission and time to breathe, loosen my vice-grip on control, and notice what comes my way.

I see divine timing as being closely intertwined with the notion that we are each on a unique spiritual path. I didn't see it this way when we (*I*) lost our keys in the ocean, or when I accepted a ride home at the end of that ill-fated first date, but I see it now.

When I criticize my own screw-ups and bad choices and think about the unplanned detours I've taken in my life, divine timing permits me to take a sky view look at my journey. I can step back and see the bigger picture. I can realize that, without making those mistakes and learning those lessons, I wouldn't be where I am now. I find this perspective liberating, not fatalistic. Divine timing has helped me to choose how I want to view the world *and* my existence in it. It is one of the most empowering tools I have discovered in my exploration of all things woo.

Don't get me wrong. I'm not about to trade in my designer frames for some sort of Pollyanna, rose-coloured glasses. Anyone who knows me knows how much I despise toxic positivity. I believe down to my core that there is no value in trying to ignore reality or reciting hollow affirmations. The "everything happens for a reason" mode of thinking can be weaponized by the toxically positive crowd: "Look on the bright side! Sure, you have cancer, but everything happens for a reason!" *Eye Roll emoji. Vomit emoji.* Sometimes things are tragic, and not everything that happens is worth celebrating.

But—more often than you might realize—it's all of the twists, turns, tragedies, and disappointments in your life that have cumulatively led you to some of the most wonderful discoveries and the most fulfilling relationships.

Mindset: Space Alien in Heels

Mindset affects our mood, outlook, motivation, and resilience levels.

As I battled daily headaches, fatigue, and my body just generally giving up on me, I continued to meditate regularly. The effects were barely noticeable at first. The struggle to feel like Kat instead of a space alien in heels was still very real.

Dr. Rose recommended that I try mantras as another easy, no-barrier way to start shifting my mindset. Not sarcastic, witty, brilliant mantras that had become my go-to, but actual, positive, talking-to-myself type of mantras. *Great. More woo.* The idea was to help transition me from my usual mode of thinking (*This is bullshit* and *I want my life back*) to something more constructive (*I can do hard things* and *things will get better*).

The first time I tried reciting a mantra to myself, the voice in my mind that took over the loudspeaker was shouting, *This is a total waste of time! It's not going to work.* Luckily, Dr. Rose had warned me that I might feel that way, so I just went with it. My mantras were along the lines of "I am strong. I can handle this. I've got this. I can do hard things."

I said the words in repetition while looking at myself in the bathroom mirror each morning. I felt like a cliché—like I belonged on some cheesy after-school TV special. At first, I *haaaaated* doing the mantras. But, as good Kats do, I followed the rules and did my homework.

Over time, I started to hear and say the words in my head throughout the day as well.

Awful court case that my coworkers said I had no chance of winning? "I've got this. If anyone can pull this one out of the fire, it's me."

CHAPTER FOUR

Face-to-face with a brutally insulting opposing counsel? "I know I'm good at this. I'm strong. He's just trying to get under my skin, and I'm not gonna let him."

Positive words started to drown out the usual critical, pessimistic Kat. "I can get through this. I can do hard things."

The words became easier for me to think and less easy to mock.

We also added gratitude to my mindset work. "Everyone has *something* to be grateful for, no matter how hard their day is or how much of a roller-coaster year they've had," Dr. Rose said when I tried to argue.

I have always been a journaler, so you'd think keeping a gratitude journal would have been relatively easy for me. Not so. My journaling practices had been sporadic at best, and my journal had become my outlet when I was feeling down in the dumps. Writing three things every day that I was grateful for seemed artificial, forced, and, well, pointless.

I was *not* grateful for where I was. I was frustrated, mad, and resentful. *Gaslighting myself and telling myself a fairytale isn't going to suddenly make it all better*, I thought.

Contrary to my own inner critic, mindset work wasn't intended to guilt or gaslight me into feeling like my problems weren't valid. Mindset practices such as mantras and gratitude practices can help open someone up to the opportunities and blessings hiding beneath seemingly insurmountable challenges.

To me, practising gratitude is related to divine timing. When you view your life through either of these lenses, it becomes easier to see that these things aren't happening *to* you, but rather, *for* you. When you can be genuinely grateful for whatever life throws at you today, and also be genuinely curious as to why these lessons are being shown to you, that's when the real magic starts to happen, my friends.

Mantras and gratitude practices have gone from being the monkey on my back to being some of my favourite go-to tools for shifting my mindset. I can now go on record and say that *any* mindset work I've done, be it spiritual or not, has been beneficial for me. As with anything related to personal development or growth, consistency has been key.

Note that I say consistency, *not* perfection. Life gets busy, and things get off track. It's the commitment to going back to your practices and re-committing yourself that matters. Even now, this many years into my journey, I still fall off the rails sometimes. I get overwhelmed by life. Caught up in the day-to-day struggles and stresses. I often need to remind myself to return to my practices and encourage myself to do the things that I *know* are going to help me feel more grounded, centred, and able to handle whatever the Universe is throwing at me.

I don't know how many weeks or months I did my mantras, meditations, and gratitude practices before I noticed a change, but there was a change. It was like a switch had been flicked. Somewhere along the line, when my day was going to shit, my inner narrative changed. Instead of the voice in my head saying, *What a mess. Holy hell, this is a disaster. What am I going to do?!* I had a louder, more positive voice in there, too, starting to drown out the negative one. *Whoa . . . that sucks, but I can get through this. I'm better off just letting it go and moving on.*

It felt a little bit like a cheat code at times. Like, all of a sudden, I could just *let it go*? Novel concept. At other times, life lifed too hard and no mantra or meditation could measure up. *Baby steps, people.*

I have slowly come to accept that the mind and the body are deeply connected. To some, that might seem like I'm just stating the obvious, but there, I've said it—Captain Obvious reporting for duty. I think it's important to acknowledge this fact, though. Many of us have grown up in a society where the mind and the body have been treated like totally separate spheres. Acknowledging the inter-relationship between the two—the "oneness" of ourselves as human beings (to use a hippie-dippie phrase that I've eventually come to love)—is, in my humble opinion, crucial to living a happy, healthy existence here on earth.

To elaborate: the connection between the mind and body is essentially a two-way street. The mind can influence the body. For example, positive thoughts can cause certain feel-good neurotransmitters like serotonin, dopamine, oxytocin, and endorphins to be released. Like-wise, the body can influence the mind. What we eat, whether (and how) we exercise, and even our posture can impact our mental state.

In truth, this two-way street is much more like a highway—nay, a complex network of highways—that exists between the brain and our immune, endocrine, and peripheral neurological systems. These systems are communicating with each other all the time. Since these chatterboxes are talking to each other whether we like it or not, the decision is yours: You can ignore this fact and pretend like the things you eat, the way you carry yourself, or the perma-scowl on your face don't matter; or, you can decide to pay attention to what your body is saying to your mind, and vice versa. I am learning that becoming more conscious of the intricate connection between our mind and our body can help us elevate our mood, our attitude, and our overall state of being.

All of that being said, as with all things in life, the decision is yours. Even a decision to do nothing is a decision—but that's a topic for another day, or a whole other book. I'm not writing this to pressure you. There is always an off-ramp if you decide this route isn't for you or you want to hit up a rest stop.

Take a Fucking Break, Kat

I kept going to my appointments, doing my mantras and meditations, and treating my assigned health and mindset practices as a set of tasks to be completed. From the outside looking in, I was keeping it all together. Nailing it, even. Inside, I felt okay some of the time, and downright depleted the rest of it.

A few months in, a work friend, Drew, who knew what I was truly going through, tried to help by challenging me to take a weekend away from it all, just for myself. He said he knew just the place: "You gotta go to Scottsdale. It's awesome. Super quick flight, great restaurants, and there's this awesome spa resort that my sister just went to and won't stop talking about."

The idea of a solo vacay at that particular point in time felt absurd. I had a mountain of work, a bunch of social obligations (stagettes and baby showers don't plan themselves) and some big upcoming hearings that I was already stressed out about . . .

Drew must have caught me in a moment of weakness, because I agreed—on the condition that he gave me all the details for where to stay, where to eat, etc. The last thing I had energy for was to go into trip-planning mode. I needed the blueprint.

A week later, I hopped on a plane to Scottsdale, Arizona (where I'd never been before), checked into the fancy spa resort Drew recommended (that I'd never heard of before), and I was ready to surrender. I'd been dreaming of the private Pilates session I'd booked for the day I arrived. Booking something like that wasn't something I'd ordinarily do for myself (Dr. Rose specifically recommended I do something that felt like I was treating myself), and I was beyond excited.

The resort was called Sanctuary. It was stunning—far more upscale than anywhere I had stayed before. Little did I realize that this place would become an actual sanctuary for me during those challenging years. After I dropped my car off with the valet, I bee-lined it for the spa to check in for my appointment, only to find out they had somehow lost my booking in their system.

"But . . . I spoke with someone. Trisha, I think? I'm sure it was booked—" I started to say, but quickly lost my words. Tears sprang to my eyes and, before I could stop them, they began streaming down my face. I swiped them away frantically. I couldn't speak because it would have surely come out in loud, hideous sobs.

My massive overreaction left the well-meaning stranger at the spa desk fumbling and desperate for ways to make up for the error. He apologized profusely while I stood there awkwardly, barely keeping it together. "We will make up for this, I promise," he said.

Evidently, the spa guy's error became an emotional tipping point following months of stress and anxiety that led up to that moment and overflowed before his horror-filled eyes. In psychology, this is often framed as a "catalyst" or "emotional release"—the small incident serves as the release valve for deeper, suppressed feelings.

Straw: one. Camel: zero.

It happens to the best of us, but I wasn't thinking about it that way at the time.

I could only nod, hold my purse close to me, and walk to the front check-in desk in humiliation to pick up my key. When I finally got myself into my room, I *fully* lost it. I threw myself down on the bed and scream-cried into a pillow. Then I settled in on the patio and put back two glasses of a tasty California chardonnay that I'd picked up along with some tamales at a nearby gourmet grocery store Drew had told me about.

Despite the rocky start, the trip did end up being refreshing. I followed the recommendations put together by my workmate (including restaurants, bars, shopping spots, art galleries, and hikes) and did my best to shake off the constant looming sadness that threatened to ruin the getaway. I also logged some solid hours by the pool, with a novel in one hand and a margarita in the other. I cried a lot (in the privacy of my own room), and rested a lot.

When I landed back at the office, I hit the ground running again. Any restfulness or energy I had stored up during my little Scottsdale escape didn't last very long. I went back to burning the candle at both ends, and it wasn't doing me any favours.

In the courtroom and the boardroom, I was classic Lawyer Kat. But sitting in Dr. Rose's office, one of the only places where I fully let my guard down, the cracks showed. It was obvious I was in pain. I was struggling. The words "taking a leave of absence" came up a few times, to my horror. They were said gently, knowing I wouldn't want to hear it.

One afternoon, I was in my office staring down a massive legal file and an equally massive migraine when Drew walked in. "Got another headache?"

I rubbed my temples. "Is it that obvious?"

He dropped into the chair across from me. "Don't worry. You still look hot."

I shot him a warning look. I wondered if he was getting used to them. Drew had become extra flirty after arranging my weekend retreat. I liked him and he was fun to have around, but he was (and always would be) very much in the friend zone.

"I think you need to take a fucking break, Kat," he said, bluntly.

"I've got too much to do," I muttered, grabbing my highlighter and turning back to the mountain of documents I needed to review. "Besides, I already took a break. Scottsdale, remember?"

"You always have too much to do."

I stared at the paper. My eyes were burning. The idea of another, more substantial break felt like a luxury I couldn't afford. But God, it sounded nice.

"Kat," he said, his voice softer. "You're allowed to take some time off. And you need to."

I nodded and kept my eyes focused (but not) on the work at hand. Drew took the hint and left the room without another word.

Just two days later, I was back in court, running on caffeine, ibuprofen, and four hours of sleep. The judge was late, and I was juggling emails on my BlackBerry under the table.

Back at the office, the pile of work on my desk had doubled. Apparently, saying, "I'm really swamped right now," translates to, "Hey, everyone—please leave me three dozen new tasks the first chance you get."

By late afternoon, I was halfway through drafting a motion when Carla popped her head into my office.

"Hey, Kat? Just wondering if you got a chance to look over—"

"I don't have time right now," I snapped, sharper than I meant to.

"Okay," she said. There was a pause before she added, "No problem," and left, the door clicking shut behind her.

CHAPTER FOUR

I stared at my screen. The words blurred. I had popped one of my prescription migraine pills, but it hadn't kicked in yet, and my headache was clawing at the edge of my skull. My highlighter slipped out of my hand and hit the floor. I didn't pick it up.

Ten minutes passed. Maybe twenty. I didn't write a word.

Finally, I saved the file, leaned back in my chair, and closed my eyes. Staring into the void and feeling more tired than I thought humanly possible were new features of my existence. I definitely didn't have those on my successful law career bingo card.

I was tired. My body was screaming at me from so many angles that it was making my head spin. Migraines. Sleep disorder. Soft tissue pain. Balance and vision problems. I'd convinced myself I just needed to take more frequent mini-breaks. More Scottsdale (or equivalent) getaways. If I took enough breathers, I could stay on the treadmill and keep moving towards my goal (making partner at the firm).

I bartered with myself. In just over a month, I'd be on a plane to Chicago for a work conference. *Perfect*, I thought. *My favourite kind of break . . . I'll be travelling, socializing, and schmoozing, all in the name of networking. This job can be rough, but it definitely has its perks.* I told myself I could hang on until then. So I did. I kept my nose to the grindstone for the next few weeks until it was time to head to Chicago.

Chicago was everything I had hoped it would be: fun American lawyers to network and hang out with, tons of great restaurants, amazing wine, fancy cocktails, piano bars, and dance clubs, followed by late-night deep-dish pizza outings. There were hungover brunches and afternoon walks along the Chicago Riverwalk with work friends, new and old. I attended several obligatory seminars and was a diligent networker. And by the end of the three-day conference, I was *spent*.

It's a good thing I planned ahead, booking myself two extra nights in Chicago, on my own dime, to rest and recover. The Yankees were playing the Chicago White Sox, and I wanted to go to the game. None of my work peeps wanted to stay an extra day to go with me, so I went on my own. Yes, I am such a baseball nerd that I will go to a Major League Baseball game in a city I don't live in, by myself. I had never been to Comiskey Park, and—bonus—because I was only looking for a single ticket, I got a fantastic seat just a few rows back from home plate.

As luck would have it, the tall, handsome drink of water that I had met during the conference texted me during the game. He lived on the south side of Chicago and offered to pick me up after the game and show me some of the local sights. After hitting up a legendary hot dog joint and a couple of bars, we ended up back at his place. The Yankees won that day, but let's just say they weren't the only ones rounding the bases.

I flew out the following morning and congratulated myself on an epic trip. I had worked hard and played hard. And I had rested— sort of. Okay, I hadn't really rested, but I *had* blown off some steam, and that's important too, I told myself. (In case you were wondering, lawyers are fabulous at justifying things to ourselves . . . one of those work skills that tends to bleed into the rest of life.)

As the plane hit the tarmac back in my hometown, I saw that I had two missed calls from my personal injury lawyer. I inhaled sharply. This was either bad news or good news. I stayed put in my seat and called him back while the rest of the passengers were hurriedly filing off the plane. He told me that my years-long insurance case surrounding the car accident had finally been resolved. I couldn't believe it. I was receiving a settlement—a good one—which certainly didn't erase the life-altering health issues I was dealing with, but it was a huge relief to suddenly have a nest egg.

I caught a cab from the airport, went home, and went straight to bed. I had been feeling fluish for the last several hours. *Maybe, just maybe, I had overdone it a bit*, I reluctantly admitted to myself. I trusted that I could sleep it off. Besides, I needed to get back into the saddle the next morning, having taken two whole extra days off work.

I couldn't shake the symptoms, but I stayed in denial about whether I had caught some kind of flu bug. I felt like garbage. I had a fever and chills, but I wasn't coughing or sneezing, so I kept on going into the office and worked my usual hours with my door closed. After a week of this, my mom and sister convinced me to go to the urgent care centre to get checked out. The right side of my torso and low back had been throbbing. This seemed odd, but my body had been home to so many different aches and pains since the car accident that I honestly hadn't thought too much of it.

A few hours later, I found myself lying on a hospital bed, with a nurse beside me putting an IV in my arm so that she could administer IV antibiotics to me. The ER doctor had poked and prodded at my torso, ordered some blood work and a CT scan.

As I lay there in the bed, feeling like a sack of shit, the doctor came back in with the results of the scan and the blood tests. "You're lucky," she said. You have a pretty serious kidney infection, but if you'd waited much longer to come in, you would have gone septic." *Septic?* I didn't understand what the term meant, but it sounded serious. Google later told me that sepsis can lead to organ damage, organ failure, septic shock or even death. *Welp. Looks like I dodged a bullet.*

The kidney infection kept me on the couch and off work for over three weeks. When you're in that state and have a lot more time on your hands than you've had in recent memory, you get to thinking.

I had done such a good job ignoring warning sign after warning sign, so it seemed the Universe had decided to turn up the volume and send me a wake-up call that I couldn't possibly ignore.

It worked. I finally sat up and took notice.

Trying to heal in secret, trying to keep all the balls in the air, it just wasn't working. Painful as that was to admit, I wasn't well. I needed help.

I was done.

"Playing like it didn't hurt" wasn't working.

Me, invincible, powerful, successful Lawyer Kat, who prided

myself on being able to do just about anything I put my mind to, was officially calling it.

It was time to figure out what the actual fuck was going on with my body and how to fix it—how to heal. And thanks to the car accident settlement, I could take the time to do so.

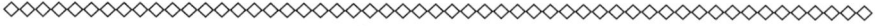

MANTRA #2:

This is bullshit.

Whyyyyyy meeeee?

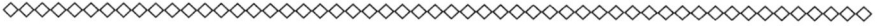

Okay, fine . . .

MANTRA #2.1:

Things can only get better.

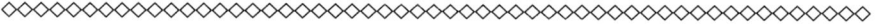

CHAPTER FIVE
Curious Kat

It turned out that I had done a great job of hiding my symptoms. When I told my firm I needed a leave of absence, most of my colleagues were shocked.

Meanwhile, I was gutted. Asking for time off was humiliating. The defeat I felt was so deep that all I could focus on was how to heal as fast as possible.

I asked my specialists in Canada if there was somewhere in the United States I could go for faster medical treatment. Don't get me wrong, I am a proud Canadian and there is nowhere I'd rather call home, but our healthcare system is, well, broken. For acute things like my kidney failure, the system worked great, and I received the care I needed exactly when I needed it. However, for anyone dealing with chronic illness or a complex set of symptoms, things didn't work quite so well. I ended up on waitlist after waitlist, most of which were several months long.

It was Dr. Rose who referred me to a team of medical professionals in New York City. They were former colleagues of hers. I accepted the referral, feeling hopeful and grateful for the prospect of finding answers, and off I went for a ten-day solo trip to New York at Christmastime.

Trip of a Lifetime

My time in New York was the stuff that rom-coms and Hallmark movies are made of. I went there to get medical treatment, and I most definitely did that. However, several other things happened that I am convinced could only take place inside the magical cloak that is New York City.

I was stopped on a street corner in midtown Manhattan at 9 a.m. by a tall, good-looking young guy in a suit who told me I was "stunning" (never had I been called this before by any man back home). When this softer-featured Keanu Reeves look-alike—whose name was, coincidentally, Keiran—heard my "cute" Canadian accent, he gave me his number and said he'd like to take me out while I was in town, if I was open to it. I obliged, and we had an incredibly fun, romantic time together.

Another night, I decided to be brave and sit by myself at a swanky hotel bar for a drink. A bunch of men circled through, standing and ordering drinks at the bar and chatting me up. A couple of them held my interest long enough that I let them buy me a drink and stay for a visit. Ultimately, it was a slightly older guy with zero game named Darren who I bonded with, and who sat with me and just talked until the wee hours. We were both healing—he from a recent divorce, and I from my concussions.

Darren was a rep for a major record label, and one of his bands was playing the next night in SoHo. It was a country band that I'd never heard of called Old Dominion. Darren humoured me and let me know they had a new album that had just come out, and they had opened and written songs for some of the big, big names in country music (singers and bands whose names I very much recognized). Despite not (yet) being a country music fan, but in the spirit of being adventurous and saying yes to new experiences, I agreed to meet Darren at the show.

I prepped for the show by watching the interview they had given that morning on Good Morning America, and downloading their album, which I listened to on the subway ride to the venue and found myself really liking.

I messaged Darren when I got off at my stop and let him know I was a few blocks away. "Is there a ticket for me at will-call?" I asked.

Darren replied, "Just let me know when you're here; someone will come up and meet you."

Much to my surprise, I was greeted at the door with a VIP lanyard and ushered directly to the green room, where I proceeded to hang out with Darren and the band before and after their set, sipping tequila and shooting the shit with them and their entourage.

After the show, the whole crew of us went for drinks at a nearby bar. Darren put me in an Uber at the end of the night to make sure I got back to my hotel safely. I woke up the next morning, got a bagel with lox and cream cheese, then walked myself to my next specialist appointment. *Was this real life?*

During my time in New York, I saw five different specialists (this sort of efficiency was unheard of back home). By far the most significant doctor I saw was a soft-spoken man named Dr. Kulkarni, a sleep specialist and neurologist. I had filled out reams of paperwork in advance of the appointment. Dr. Rose had sent my medical records for him to review. I sat nervously in the exam room waiting for the doctor to come in. Within ten minutes of his arrival, and after asking me just a few brief clarifying questions, Dr. Kulkarni had diagnosed my sleep disorder—a rare offshoot of narcolepsy caused by a dysregulated neuropeptide in my brain called orexin—and explained my treatment options.

The whole thing felt somewhat anti-climactic, especially since my symptoms had been so vexing to the doctors back home. Wasn't there more digging to do? More sleuthing required? I asked Dr. Kulkarni if he was sure about the diagnosis. He smiled gently and assured me that, although the sleep disorder I had was relatively rare, this was a very clear case and he had encountered two or three people with the same disorder during his career.

Seeing the New York physicians had armed me with the information and diagnoses I needed to help further my medical treatment back home. That trip got me through the bottleneck that I had been trapped in, but it was not a silver bullet. I had a lot of healing work to do before I could get back to any semblance of normal life or work.

I spent the next ten or so months doing all manner of rehab activities and resting my body, giving it the dedicated time to heal that I had previously deprived it. I was, in a way, hibernating. Hiding. I felt like a shell of myself. Who was I without work? With high-achieving Lawyer Kat sitting on the bench, who was the "me" that was left? These were questions I was reluctant to examine or even acknowledge, but they were there, lurking beneath the surface, to be sure.

Back to Work

After many months of dedicated rehab, I was starting to get my groove back. I began rattling the fence and demanding to be taken off the bench and put back in the game. It was, I decided, time to take my life back.

I paid for an occupational therapist (OT), Suzanne, to help me get back to work without reinjuring myself or causing any self-inflicted setbacks. The return to work was agonizingly slow . . . and awkward. My colleagues were tiptoeing around me like I was a fragile flower, unsure whether they could ask for my help on a file, and nervous that they would be overburdening me if they did.

MANTRA #3:

Start slooow.

Suzanne forced me to ask for the accommodations I needed. One of the accommodations was to *start slow*. Before all of this, I didn't have a "slow" setting. As per the schedule that she had worked up, I went in for a few hours here and there at first. The goal was to build up to part-time, which is kind of comical because there's no such thing as being a part-time litigator; you're either on the case or you're not. When the phone rings, the trajectory of the file hinges on your answer. It is next to impossible to show up without showing all the way up.

But by 2017 (five years after the car accident concussion, and seven years after the bike accident concussion), I was sick of being tired and tired of being sick. So I was willing to give the gradual return to work a try.

I had been so consumed the past few years, trying to keep my health issues a secret while simultaneously trying to kill it at my job. As I was coming out of survival mode and a period of instability in my life unlike any other, a dormant but nagging sensation surfaced: I realized that I was searching for clarity and direction. What was next for me? When would my other mile markers finally happen? I wanted so badly to move out of this painful chapter and on to sunnier days.

A friend had told me about a psychic she'd been to named Marni Fordham (*"She's the real deal, Kat, I swear."*) I had always been curious about psychics, but never saw myself as the type of person who would go to one. I was too serious, too logical, too grounded in reality. And psychics were anything *but*. But for whatever reason, on that day, in that frame of mind, I felt desperate. And curious. *To hell with it.* I booked in for a psychic reading. If it turned out to be a bunch of nonsense, I didn't have to tell anyone I'd even gone. It could be my little secret.

Before going in for my session, I did what I had seen people on TV do when they were skeptical like me and about to visit the *Long Island Medium*: I was careful to hide anything that might lead the psychic to answers about me. I tried to make sure my appearance didn't give away any clues. I still looked roughly like the same person I had always been, only now I was a little worse for wear due to all the health stuff.

I arrived at the psychic's apartment, and when she greeted me at the door, I wasn't sure if it was Marni or a roommate—she looked surprisingly normal. She was wearing jeans and a cute, flowy top. "Hi, I'm Katherine. I'm here to see—"

"Hi!" she said, before I could finish. "It's me, I'm Marni. Come in, come in!" She led me into her apartment and motioned for me to sit down at her dining room table. "I'm just brewing some tea. You want some?" she asked warmly on her way to the kitchen.

"Um, sure, thanks!" I said, looking around at the space. Apart from the beaded curtain thingy in one of the doorways, and the Buddha statues and crystals on the side tables and windowsill, her place looked fairly unremarkable. It was bright and airy, and didn't feel like the stereotypical candlelit fortune teller's parlour, with window coverings on all the windows and a crystal ball on the table.

Marni brought me my tea and then sat down kitty-corner from me at the table. She had me place my hand on the deck of tarot cards (to infuse them with my energy), and explained that the card spread would form the basis of the reading, and she would also receive messages from my "team," which she would relay to me.

She gave me what sounded like her standard spiel and told me that she considered herself an intuitive, not a psychic. "Look, I'm not going to try to predict your future. I'm going to use my intuitive abilities to tune into the messages from the Universe and convey those to you. You are still a human being with free will. What you do with the messages is ultimately up to you, I'm just here to be the conduit."

Marni dealt the cards out onto the table and studied them for a couple of minutes. She closed her eyes and started relaying messages she said she was receiving from "Spirit" (her word). Much to my chagrin, they were all about work.

"I am being told that you need to slow down," she said with her eyes still closed. "Does that make sense to you?"

"Uhh, no. That can't be right," I argued. "I'm on a gradual return to work right now . . . I already *did* slow down, and I'm just now getting back into the swing of things. I'm trying to gear back up, actually." *Sheesh.*

She wasn't phased. This wasn't her first rodeo. "Well, your spirit guides want you to slow down even more."

*A **spirit guide** is said to be a soul who has learned all of their lessons and lived all of their lives on this earthly plane (and maybe other realms and planes too), such that they have nothing left to learn here, and so they are dedicated to guiding other souls through their journeys.*

It was already hard enough to be only half-time at work. (*I dare anyone else to try to be half a lawyer!*) It just doesn't work that way. And I was doing my best. *Spirit Guides?* I bit my tongue and looked away to hide my rolling eyes. Maybe this was a mistake. What was I even doing here?!

Surely sensing my annoyance, she asked, "Do *you* have any questions you want me to ask your Spirit Guides?"

I had nothing *but* questions. I had a list of milestones still ahead of me, with marriage and kids being the most important, and as of that moment, I wasn't even really dating anyone seriously. "When am I going to meet someone?"

She smiled and nodded, surely having been asked the same question countless times. "Ah, yes. Okay. Let's look at that." She began to describe the man I was going to marry. "He will be very gentlemanly . . . He will be well-dressed . . . He will make you feel cared for and loved . . . He'll be passing through town, on his way to somewhere else, when you meet . . . he doesn't live here . . . I see you two travelling the world together . . ."

She went on, and I listened. Despite all the doubts I had inside about how real this reading was, I desperately wanted Marni to be right. I was ready to find love and settle down.

Less than two months later, I met my future husband. He showered me with love and affection. He lived somewhere else and was indeed passing through when we connected. We travelled together. Almost two years to the day after meeting him, I married him.

After that reading, I spent some time researching spirit guides. I read that they can show up in lots of ways, presenting opportunities in the form of weird coincidences (or *synchronicities*).

Synchronicities *are meaningful, seemingly related coincidences that lack a clear cause-and-effect connection (a concept developed by psychologist Carl Jung).*

They sometimes send messages to you through symbols, numbers, and other signs. At other times, they will present you with obstacles or challenges if there is a particular lesson that your soul wants to learn or work on in this lifetime. I will admit that I like the idea that "the Universe is rigged in my favour." It's got a divine-timing quality to it, and has since become one of my favourite sayings. The idea that there is a whole spiritual network working behind the scenes and conspiring in my favour is not only comforting, but has helped me open up to experiences, opportunities, and teachings that I might have previously seen as disappointments or tragedies.

Whether I manifested my husband, or my Spirit Guides were right on the money, I had found love, and I was happy.

I also decided that slowing down at work would come in the form of moving to his city—a smaller, sleepier place on an island where I would primarily work remotely. It was a solid idea. In reality, however, I still ended up working crazy hours and billing more (and earning more) that year than I ever had before.

In 2019, I became pregnant. Let me tell you, saying positive affirmations in the mirror or mantras throughout the day while you feel like a beached whale is not easy. I kept up with my meditations, though, more out of habit than anything.

I gave birth to a beautiful baby girl during the first week of pandemic lockdowns. I loved her more than I ever realized I could love someone. As she grew and began toddling about, she only became more interesting. I loved her baby talk. She would say "lello" instead of "yellow" and "smoolie" instead of "smoothie. "What tha heck!" was her favourite thing to shout when something happened that she didn't like. During one particular kitchen dance party, she said to me, "Mummy, giggle your butt!" (She wanted me to wiggle my butt with her as we were dancing.) She was all that was right with the world.

My husband and I were another story. Any adoration and love between us had disappeared as quickly as it had appeared. Our arguments left me feeling like a failure as a wife and a mother. We argued over money, schedules, parenting, and just about everything else. And things got mean. I felt ashamed and guilty, as if the whole situation was my fault. (*I hadn't yet been diagnosed with postpartum anxiety and depression, and I didn't yet know what gaslighting was.*)

I turned back to journaling and writing poetry—anything I could think of to help release the feelings that were suffocating me.

I remember admitting to my friend Kyla that I was struggling. She was a personal trainer I had worked with in the months leading up to my wedding. She was one of the first people I truly connected with after moving cities to live with my (then) fiancé. I kept training with Kyla after the wedding, during my pregnancy and throughout my year-long maternity leave. She was calm, chill, and fun, and not at all intimidating considering her bikini-perfect body. We had become good friends, and I felt like I could tell her anything without being judged.

Unbeknownst to me before I logged onto our virtual coffee date that day, Kyla had explored quite a bit of woo herself. I knew that she had done her yoga teacher training and had more recently become a breathwork practitioner (whatever that meant). During our coffee date, she chatted about several other very spiritual topics, including oracle cards.

"Could you pull some oracle cards for me?" I asked, loving the idea of getting a reading from one of my favourite people. My baby napped nearby, and my husband was working in the other room. "Omigosh, I would love to, Kat. Let me go grab some decks."

"Do you know what you want to ask?"

"Mmhmm," I nodded.

"Okay, think about the question in your mind, but don't say it out loud. Just hold the energy of the question and ask Spirit for guidance," she said as she shuffled each of the five decks we had decided to use. I did as she said. My question was: *Is it the right time for a career shift?*

Kyla pulled a card from each deck for me. She explained the cards as she pulled them and read out the passages contained in the respective guidebooks. The cards delivered strong, clear messages about transition, change, and growth.

I could tell that Kyla believed in what she was doing. And because I believed in Kyla, the reading gave me hope. It also reminded me there were people in the world who didn't make me feel like a shameful excuse of a mother, a wife, or a human when they were around.

A few weeks after doing the oracle cards with Kyla, I applied for (and ultimately landed) a legal counsel job with the government. It offered better work-life balance, the ability to pick my child up from daycare every day, and evenings at home. I called Kyla the day I landed the job.

"Congrats, Kat!" she exclaimed. "See? You manifested it!" Whether I had or not, whether the woo was working or not, I happily took the win.

After that, life kicked into another gear. I had a new job I loved, a daughter I adored, a great group of friends, and even though I was pretty sure my marriage was falling apart, the rest of my life seemed to be on the up-and-up.

I added books that were more woo to my reading list. The Curious Kat version of me wanted to know more. Learn more. Find more answers. I read *May Cause Miracles* and *The Universe Has Your Back* (both by Gabby Bernstein), *You Are a Badass* (Jen Sincero), *Untamed* (Glennon Doyle), *The Surrender Experiment* (another great one by Michael Singer), *Big Magic* (Elizabeth Gilbert), *Radical Acceptance* (Tara Brach), and *The Way of Integrity* (Martha Beck).

I also found myself doing guided meditations and saying my mantras and positive affirmations more often. If there was any chance I had manifested my new job, why stop now?

Oracle Cards

After my reading with Kyla, I got an oracle deck of my own. I wanted to play with them, learn about them, and see where it took me. Oracle cards are super approachable and accessible for beginners. The decks usually come with a guidebook where the author of the deck has sketched out what the meaning, intention, and/or message behind each card is, or what it might reveal about the situation you find yourself in, or the question you posed to Spirit (now my word) before you pulled the card.

Before I pull a card from my oracle deck, I knock on the deck a few times with my "door-knocking" knuckles. This is supposed to push out any old energy that may still be in the deck from the last person who used it, or the last time I pulled a card. Then I hold the deck and sit for a few quiet moments, infusing the deck with my energy. Then I either spread the cards on a table and choose one that I feel drawn to or, more likely, I shuffle the deck, and just keep shuffling and shuffling until one card jumps out or falls out on its own . . . this is the card that was meant for me.

There are many ways to pull cards. I tend to do one-card pulls, but you can also do spreads where you pull multiple cards. Some popular three-card spreads include: past/present/future, situation/obstacle/ outcome, what you know/what you don't know/how to move forward.

Tarot Cards

Reading tarot cards requires more knowledge and understanding of the cards' images and what they represent. There are seventy-eight cards, each having its own meaning, plus reversal meanings (when you pull a card and the image is upside-down).

You don't have to learn all of the cards by heart to do a tarot reading; you can do a simple three- or five-card spread similar to an oracle spread. Some tarot decks also come with guidebooks, which can come in handy if you're doing your own reading or still learning.

Personally, if I'm going to do a tarot reading, I like to have an experienced tarot reader perform the reading for me. It's worth splurging on from time to time. I can and do pull oracle cards on my own, but navigating the less straightforward messages that can be encoded in full-blown tarot card spreads like the *Celtic Cross* can benefit from an expert perspective—someone who is steeped in the tarot tradition and used to reading the cards in conjunction with one another.

Spiritual Words & Titles

As an English Lit major, lawyer, poetry lover, and general lifelong word nerd, I will be the first to acknowledge that words and titles matter. Earning the title of Lawyer changed how I felt about myself. Later, so did the label of Wife, and then Mom. When people referred to me as ill or injured, that also affected how I felt.

I think we can acknowledge that plenty of people can use different words to describe the same concept, and that some people use the same word or title but ascribe dramatically different meanings to that term. As we like to say in the legal field, "reasonable minds can differ."

Titles and labels in the woo realm—terms like Spirit, God, Universe, Source—can make people feel a lot of different ways. As far as I'm concerned, the main thing that matters about spiritual titles is how *you* use them and what meaning *you* attribute to them. It's choose your own adventure, and I'm not here to judge.

The word God can have many associations and connotations. People who have been raised in faith in Western society may reserve the title solely for the Christian God. There are, of course, many religions and many gods. Some religions have dozens of gods of their own.

The word God had specific religious connotations for me growing up in a Christian-lite sort of household, and the term doesn't resonate for me when I'm speaking about a broader non-denominational spiritual context. And so began my search for a different, more neutral-feeling word that could capture the concept of the omnipotent, omnipresent, benevolent force that I believe exists within and around all of us.

Universe is a term that I like and one that I use often. I like the sense of vastness and mystique it carries with it. It also feels a bit sassy, like you can never quite pin it down or hem it in—it's the *Universe*, after all, so don't even try.

Now (years after my first psychic reading), I've gotten comfortable with the terms Spirit and Source, among others. Words and titles that used to make me roll my eyes now feel fairly neutral and applicable to lots of different contexts.

Cheat Codes, Please and Thank You

I felt like a toddler getting my first real taste of sugar. I was hooked. If there was a tool, a cheat code, a secret password, or a fast lane to feeling better, I wanted to have it, know it, or be on it.

Woo Kat and Woo Google spent a lot more time together as we researched the good, bad, and ugly of the metaphysical world. Some of it sounded like BS. And some of it sounded like answers to questions I'd been asking for a long time.

I learned about various woo tools (aka metaphysical or divination tools) that people use to find their answers. Oracle cards were one of them. That made sense to me, as did tarot cards. Turns out there are lots of divination tools out there besides just those.

CHAPTER FIVE

I came across an article about **pendulums**. The theory is that you can ask a yes or no question to the pendulum, and it will swing in a particular direction and give you a binary answer. Simple. Easy. (*And most likely bogus*, I thought.) I'd seen a pendulum used before and assumed the person holding it was imperceptibly moving the pendulum to get the answers they wanted. The whole thing had high-school-Ouija-board-sleepover vibes all over it.

Fast forward to me standing in a metaphysical store, browsing the pendulum selection. I was drawn to a rather delicate, small-ish turquoise crystal one, so I picked it up and held it in my hand. The proprietor (whom I specifically noticed was fairly mainstream in appearance) saw me looking and came over to see if I needed help. I candidly asked, "So, do these things actually work?" I did my best to ask the question without a hint of judgment or holier-than-thouness.

She smirked and said, "Yep! I was surprised, too." Apparently, she picked up on the fact that I had little experience with it.

I wanted to try it out. I was still as skeptical as I had been during my first intuitive reading, but the curiosity and quest for answers drowned out the snarky, logical voice in my head.

The store owner showed me how to use the pendulum. I decided it was worth a try, so I made my purchase and took it home.

The next morning, while I was sitting having my coffee, I pulled out the pendulum, eager to see what kind of answers it would give me. I followed the shop owner's instructions exactly. I didn't want to allow any bias to interfere with the process. *I need to know if this thing is real.*

I held the pendulum chain in my right hand and placed my left hand a couple of inches below the bottom of the pendulum. I asked the pendulum to "show me a *yes*," as directed by the friendly proprietor. It swung back and forth, towards me and away from me. Then I asked it to "show me a *no*," and it swung the other way—side to side. I blinked, squinted, and watched in a state of semi-disbelief with my eyes going back and forth between the pendulum and the hand that was holding the pendulum chain. I wasn't moving a muscle—at least I was pretty sure I wasn't. I was trying my damnedest not to. But the pendulum *was* moving. I needed more evidence, so I kept asking questions.

"Is my name Kat?" I asked.

It swung back and forth, towards me and then away from me. *Yes.*

"Is my name Taylor Swift?" It swung left to right, side to side. *No.* I spent God-only-knows-how-long asking it yes-or-no questions, all of which I knew the answers to, and it continued to get them right.

"Holy shit," I whispered. I had so many questions . . . real questions! So I started asking the real ones. I was floored by some of the answers.

My phone buzzed, and I remembered that it was a workday and I needed to get going. I chugged the rest of my lukewarm coffee and hopped in the car. On my drive in, I thought about the answers Spirit had given me through the pendulum and wondered whether there were any work friends I could talk to about this who wouldn't judge me. I was still new-ish at the job, and didn't want to risk it, so I decided to keep it to myself.

Muscle testing works on a similar premise to pendulum testing. You ask a question and then use one of the well-known physical tests to see if your body and spirit are telling you that it's a yes or a no.

Some of the most basic ways to muscle-test are by making a circle with the thumb and a finger on one hand, then with a single straight finger on your other hand, try to break the circle. If the circle holds, that's typically a yes. If the circle is easy to break, that's a no. Another similar way to do this is by making two circles and seeing if one of the circles breaks (or not) when you ask the question.

Muscle testing can be a good way of confirming the answer you received through a pendulum test, particularly since pendulum testing results can be very subtle for some people.

Fast forward to me back at the metaphysical store the following weekend, fresh off the high of my recent pendulum sessions and all the insights and confirmations that I felt Spirit was giving me. I wanted to know more, even though the voice of logic-driven Lawyer Kat was in the back of my mind, telling me to "get a grip."

I stood in front of a table full of **crystals**.

"How did it go with the pendulum?" The familiar shop owner asked as she walked over. I filled her in on my experience, trying not to appear too excited, an easy mark.

"They're so pretty," I mused as I gazed at the crystals.

"And powerful," she nodded. "Some people use them for their transformative, healing qualities. Different crystals hold different energetic frequencies, and can be supportive for dealing with different issues and ailments."

I said nothing. I was too busy wondering if I'd officially lost it. Was I going to grow old in a house cluttered with crystals (and maybe twenty or thirty cats), to which my daughter was too embarrassed to visit? *What on earth was happening to respectable, sensible Lawyer Kat?*

"I've done some reading about crystals," I said. "They're considered pseudoscience."

Woo Google had also given me links to publications acknowledging that they may offer a placebo effect, especially when used in conjunction with meditation or mindfulness practices.

I secretly wanted the shop lady to find a hole in my argument. Instead, unphased as always, she started handing me crystals, talking me through each of them and what they're used for. Some people meditate with them, some carry them everywhere they go, some put them on necklaces as pendants, or wear beaded crystal bracelets.

Crystals' atoms are arranged in repeating patterns. They electromagnetically interact with physical forms of energy (mechanical, thermal, electrical), and some crystals even generate an electric charge when pressure is applied, which is a prime example of why quartz is used in watches, electronics, and sensors. Other crystals can produce an electric charge with temperature changes.

Some people are drawn to the idea that the energy frequencies emitted by different crystals can affect our energetic field, and that we can exchange or absorb a crystal's energy by holding it or keeping it nearby.

"Which crystals are you drawn to?" she asked. "It's perfectly okay to let your intuition and curiosity guide you . . . In fact, I recommend it," she said, smiling.

I picked up a rose quartz crystal shaped like a little pyramid.

"Aww, such a good choice! That one is all about love. Love for others and yourself," she said, nodding thoughtfully. *I could certainly use a little more self-love and a little less self-judgment*, I thought to myself. I picked up a few more, and she continued to name the properties of the various pretty crystals. Then she gave me a little card outlining the meanings and properties of some of the most common crystals.

Agate	Grounding, stabilizing, protective, and healing. Enhances concentration and connection to nature.

Amethyst	Has calming properties and is believed to enhance intuition, promote emotional balance, and aid in sleep and relaxation. Used for healing, purifying, and enhancing willpower.
Carnelian	Associated with passion, motivation, creativity, confidence, and joy.
Citrine	Promotes positivity, joy, and creativity. Attracts abundance, prosperity, and success. Known as a stone of manifestation.
Fluorite	Good for clearing negative energy, enhancing mental clarity, focus, and decision-making. It is often used in meditation and study.
Jade	Associated with good luck and prosperity. It is believed to attract abundance and success, and promote harmony and balance.
Lapis Lazuli	Stone of wisdom, intuition, and self-awareness. Enhances creativity, improves communication, and deepens spiritual connection.

Malachite	Strength, courage, and abundance, reduces stress and tension and balances the mind and body. (*Where was this seven years ago when I needed it??*)
Moonstone	Intuition, emotional balance, and nurturing energy. Surrender, acceptance, patience.
Obsidian	Shields against negativity; promotes emotional healing and groundedness.
Quartz	Clear quartz is known as the stone of clarity. Often called the "master healer," it can amplify energy, intention, and healing. Used for clarity, focus, and spiritual growth.
Ruby	Passion, vitality, courage, strength. Associated with the heart chakra.
Rose Quartz	Unconditional love, self-love, forgiveness, harmony in relationships.
Tiger's Eye	Known for protection and grounding, promotes confidence, courage, and strength. It can help with focus and clarity.

Turquoise	Symbol of friendship and loyalty. Fosters harmony and understanding in relationships. Also good for soothing emotions and bringing luck.
Unakite	Heart healing, growth, and transformation. Promotes balance between the heart and mind, facilitating a harmonious relationship between emotions and rational thought

A Note on Chakras and Crystals

If you are doing some focused healing around a particular chakra (heart healing or solar plexus healing, for example), you can choose stones that are associated with that chakra's colour. The solar plexus chakra, being yellow, means citrine or amber or another yellow/golden-hued stone would be a good choice. If you are hoping to open up your connection to spirit, you would focus on the crown chakra (associated with violet or white), and you might want to go with a moonstone or an amethyst.

I grabbed a couple of other stones that I felt drawn to (moonstone and howlite) and decided to call it a day.

That night, when I was at home, I followed the instructions the shop owner had given me about cleansing my crystals. It turned out there were a few steps involved in activating my crystals. Google was helpful and gave me some tips to follow as well.

Half-doubting whether these steps would do anything, I decided it couldn't hurt, and went through the motions.

Step 1. Cleanse: Before doing anything else, I was supposed to cleanse my crystals. Like everything we encounter in our day-to-day life, a crystal may still have energy (positive or negative) attached to it from the other people who have held it before me and from the places it has been. There are a few ways to cleanse crystals, including: physically cleaning them with water or salt water (but check first because some kinds of stones shouldn't be wet); visualizing water running over the crystal (*seriously?*); using sea salt; or even by placing them close to certain other stones, some of which are known to be cleansing and purifying (like clear quartz and selenite).

Step 2. Charge: In woo communities, charging crystals is a common practice thought to focus and enhance the crystal's energy. Moonlight (particularly under a full moon) is said to be excellent for charging crystals. The energy of the moon is feminine and is said to be particularly helpful for spiritual and emotional healing. Alternatively, sunlight is also good, but is considered more of a masculine energy and better suited for programming your crystals, or when you are approaching an endeavour that requires greater effort or momentum. When I was starting, I placed my stones on a windowsill during the full moon.

Step 3. Program: Crystals are said to be more powerful when we imbue them with intention. So I sat with my crystals and set an intention with each of them. With my moonstone, I set the intention to surrender and do my best to accept whatever the Universe's plan was for me. *Take your hands off the steering wheel and release your grip for once, Kat.* With the howlite, I set an intention of seeing things clearly and calmly, and asking for patience in the face of life's challenges. And with the rose quartz, I borrowed a prayer from Gabby Bernstein's book *May Cause Miracles*, and chose the following intention: during difficult moments or times of frustration or anger, I would call upon the loving energy of rose quartz and say to myself, "I choose to see love instead of this."

After I'd done all the steps, the crystals typically sat on my bookshelf or my bedside table. I'd set them outside or on the windowsill during full moons. And from time to time, I used them during my meditations—I would hold them in my hands while I meditated, and I swear that when I had the crystals in hand, I dropped in *hard*. I would quickly sink into a deep meditative state, and sometimes be a little dazed at the end of a sitting. I recall having some big revelations (or "downloads" as some people refer to them in spiritual circles) during those crystal-charged meditations. Call it woo, call it the placebo effect, all I know is that I felt dialled in to Spirit on those occasions, and I left my meditation cushion feeling like a different person than when I had sat down.

Over time, I went back for more crystals, feeling drawn to different stones and always feeling like there was a reason I would benefit from having them nearby. I had a few big chunkers, but a lot of my crystals were small and pocket-sized, and I started carrying one or two of them around with me in my purse or in a pocket when I felt like I needed a little boost or an extra reminder of the intentions I had set.

Crystals over Coffee

At some point during my exploration of all these new "woo tools," I set a coffee date with a friend whom I hadn't seen in forever.

This friend, Abigail, worked with my friend Rosie. She was a few years younger than me and had also suffered a catastrophically disruptive concussion that had interrupted her otherwise burgeoning professional career. Abigail isn't in law, though; she's an actuary (aka: someone who is freakishly good at math and makes a career of it). Shared experiences around traumatic brain injuries aren't the most awesome reason for making a new friend, but we could relate to each other in a way that few others could, and our friendship stuck.

That day, we ended up having a long talk about one of her family members who had been struggling and had been starting to investigate meditation and other spiritual tools as a way to help him cope and make sense of the jumbled mess he felt like his life had become.

I confessed to my experiences with meditation, psychics, pendulums, and now, crystals. I remember holding my breath, unsure of what her reaction was going to be.

She wanted to know more. "I've always been kind of curious about all that 'woo-woo' sort of stuff! But in a profession like mine, that sort of thing is pretty frowned upon, and I don't have any other friends who are into it. I love that you're actually investigating it." I sipped my coffee and breathed an invisible sigh of relief. "I've always wanted to know what crystals do! What would you suggest for this kind of situation? I'd love to mail him a little crystal and a note of encouragement for everything he's going through."

I delighted in the opportunity to be a mini-expert and give her my suggestions (amethyst and rose quartz were at the top of my list on this particular occasion, in case you're curious). I also encouraged her to go to one of the metaphysical stores in town, feel into it, and see which crystals were calling to her.

It felt so nice to not only *not* be judged (*by a square, professional peer, no less*), but also to have been genuinely helpful to a friend who was looking for some guidance. Maybe Woo Kat wasn't totally losing her shit after all.

Shadow Work

As my sweet daughter grew and blossomed, my marriage had done the exact opposite. After a lot of soul searching and therapy, I had pulled the trigger on a separation, and we were indeed headed for divorce. Ending a relationship that I had expected to last a lifetime brought up a lot of emotions for me, and I felt a lot of shame and guilt for my "failed" marriage. Enter: shadow work.

It's human nature to want to avoid uncomfortable feelings, thoughts, and memories. Just like the baby who puts their hands over their eyes and is convinced that you have disappeared, those dark pieces of ourselves don't just disappear because we've decided not to look at them. Oh no. They live on, silently, stealthily, within our subconscious, and they have a much greater effect on our day-to-day behaviours than we may realize or like to acknowledge. So when I came across shadow work in my research one night, it just made sense.

Shadow work involves looking within oneself to learn about and embrace the hidden, scary, unknown thoughts, feelings, and pain that exist inside each of us. It's the process of exploring and integrating those repressed or ignored aspects of ourselves that we see as negative or undesirable.

The thing about shadows—both physical and metaphorical—is that every human has them. At their core, our shadows represent our unmet needs, unfulfilled wishes, unresolved conflicts, and unlived desires.

Anyone can deny, hide, or reject those parts of themself. Or, they can see and love themselves as a whole—shadows and light—and learn to love even the wounded, messy parts we once deemed unlovable.

I remember trying to squash negative thoughts about the life I thought I was building. *Was I a bad wife? Did my husband think I was a bad mother? Was I doing enough to hold up my part of the relationship? Was I failing?* I tried to double down on positive affirmations as if they were intended to be positive delusions, but—shocker—it didn't work.

What I've since learned is that, as cliché as it sounds, without the dark, there is no light. Without sadness, happiness loses its meaning. And as much as I wish it were so, denial is not a spiritual tool. If I couldn't love myself unconditionally—my whole self—who was I to love someone else that way?

◇◇

MANTRA #4:

I love this part of me.

◇◇

To do shadow work, you have to be willing to go inward, and you have to be willing to go deep. I was told it would feel hard, especially at first, and it was. But, in time, I became more comfortable with my shadows. I acknowledged my quirks, my flaws, and—gulp—my mistakes. First with tears. Then with f-bombs. Then with love.

With shadow work, you grow to have more compassion for yourself when you royally muck things up. Once your eyesight adjusts to the darker hue, you'll see that it's a beautiful place. I recommend that anyone and everyone come visit.

There are so many ways to do shadow work:

1. Journaling: Writing freely and honestly about your innermost fears, or moments of anger or shame. Try to write without censoring yourself. Let it all spill out. No one else will see it, and you don't ever have to look at it again if you don't want to. Just. Write. This process can be cathartic and deeply insightful.

2. Guided Meditations and Visualizations: You know I love my guided meditations, but in the beginning, I didn't realize they could be used for shadow work, too. Pull out your phone and search "shadow work" on your favourite meditation app, and you're sure to find a guided meditation that will help with this. If you want to do a self-guided meditation, I suggest visualizing yourself in a safe space and inviting your shadow self to reveal itself. Sit down with your shadow, ask it what it's afraid of, what motivates it, and what it needs to feel safe and loved. In short: make friends with your shadow.

3. Identifying Triggers: Notice when certain situations or people provoke strong emotional responses in you. When you have a quiet moment, reflect on why these triggers affect you and how they might be connected to unresolved issues from your past. Pull out that journal again. It's amazing how the act of pen on paper (real pen and paper, not just fingers on a keyboard if you can manage it) can help you process those sticky, icky feelings.

4. Inner Child Work: Connecting with your inner child (not an actual child, of course, but a theoretical representation of yourself when you were young who suffered childhood traumas that have stuck with you into adulthood) through meditation or therapy can be an amazing way of offering yourself support and compassion. By asking your inner child what they needed back then to feel safe and loved, and by providing that to them now, you can do some powerful healing. To speak to your inner child essentially means to reconnect with that vulnerable little kid inside you who was perhaps punished or silenced when they just needed to be heard or hugged.

5. Practising Self-Compassion: Acknowledging and accepting your shadow traits without judgment—while easier said than done, it is doable if you commit to doing it. There are some handy-dandy mantras and some great self-compassion resources available out there, so go take a look. (If you're interested in this, check out the work of Kristin Neff, Ph.D.).

6. Pay Attention to Your "Mirrors": This one's a biggie for me. Take note when certain qualities in others irritate you or get you feeling all judgy. Oftentimes, it's because these very traits might reflect aspects of your own shadow. Brutal, I know. But woo can be used for tough love, too.

7. Therapy or Coaching: Working with someone who is trained in shadow work can be super valuable as you navigate this unfamiliar part of your inner landscape. They can provide a safe space while helping you uncover deeper issues and work through challenging emotions in a way that feels sustainable and healthy, as opposed to overwhelming and, well, terrifying.

8. Creative Expression: Think drawing, painting, music, singing, and writing—all of these creative activities can become outlets that can help you to explore and express your shadow. This can also be thought of as creative spirituality.

Creative Kat

For a long, long time, I told myself and truly believed that I wasn't a creative person. I was the logic-driven, perfect-student, future lawyer, star athlete, Kat. No artists here. Art and creativity were fluffy and useless. Sound familiar?

You may or may not have told yourself something along these lines, or maybe worse, been told this by parents, friends, or teachers. Well, I'm calling bullshit. I have come to learn that we are *all* creative, just as we are all spiritual in our own ways.

You may not have allowed yourself to tap into this part of yourself before, but believe me when I tell you that it's there. I've never painted, and I don't draw. I don't know how to play any musical instruments. Creativity wasn't exactly encouraged in my household growing up. It was treated more as a frivolous extra-curricular as opposed to a necessary element and expression of my humanity. Spiritual practices do not have to look or sound a certain way. There are things that you, almost certainly, are already doing in your life that have a very spiritual element to them, whether you've realized it (yet) or not.

Do you have any creative passions? Practices? Inklings, even? For many years, I have written poetry in my journal (what I considered to be embarrassingly bad, cringey poetry that I would be mortified for anyone to read or for it ever to see the light of day). This has been an off-and-on practice for me. Sometimes I only cracked open that journal and spilled my poetic guts into it when I was depressed, homesick, or going through a break-up.

Nowadays, poetry is one of my most cherished practices. Sometimes I intentionally set aside time for it. Other times, it grabs hold of me and stops me in my tracks, and I pull over to the side of the road to feverishly type the words into my phone as they tumble out of me, trying my best to capture them before they vanish into the ether.

I once read a quote by Elizabeth Gilbert in her book, *Big Magic*: "When an idea finally realizes that you're oblivious to its message, it will move on to someone else." Something about that just landed for me. And if it was true, I had no intention of letting those ideas fly away, onto someone else.

A poem can be spurred by a feeling, an image, or something I am struck by in nature. Sometimes a word or a phrase just pops into my head (a download, if you will) and I know it is asking to be written. Sometimes a poem comes out fully formed, and it feels like I am just the conduit. More often, they start as fragments, pieces floating around that I pluck out of the air before they escape my grasp and float away forever.

Those who woo often feel strongly that channelling their creativity connects them more deeply to God or Spirit, letting Spirit speak through them and whatever creative goodies are flowing at the time. There are so many ways to tap into your spiritual self through creative activities. Whether it is painting, drawing, singing, dancing, knitting, cooking, gardening, playing an instrument, writing, or sculpting.

Do something, anything, that nourishes your soul. Do it by yourself, if that feels easier, to start. Dance alone in your kitchen. Sing at the top of your lungs in your car. Stop by the art supply store and pick up the materials for a little painting or crafting project. Let whatever is inside of you come out. Express without filtering. No one else needs to see it . . . including you. (You're allowed to put it in a drawer and never look at it again if you don't want to.) It's not the final product or the end result that matters—for any perfectionists like myself, this takes some getting used to.

Practice detaching from the outcome. It doesn't matter if that rose bush thrives. It doesn't matter if you muck up the painting or if the poem is cringey. What matters is that you're doing it. What matters most is how you *feel* while you're doing it.

For me, detaching from the outcome and becoming immersed in the process is the key. It's more about the process, the journey, than the destination. Cheesy? Yes. True? Also yes.

Any discussion of creative spirituality would be incomplete without a mention of *The Artist's Way*, by Julia Cameron. *The Artist's Way* is a book, a program, a method that encourages burgeoning, self-doubting or blocked creatives to set aside the fear, the self-judgment and the obsessive belief that what you are creating is not "good enough."

Two of Cameron's core practices have attained widespread popularity: **morning pages** and **artist dates**. Morning pages is a practice of writing (handwriting) three pages every morning to get the mental chatter "out of your system." The idea being that, by spewing out everything (negative, positive, inane, insightful), you can get to the other side of it and not stay bogged down by it. You can get past the judgment and the self-censoring and make space for your creativity to flow, unimpeded. Artist dates are a weekly practice of taking yourself on a solo excursion or activity intended to cultivate inspiration. My current go-to artist date is doing a tea walk down to my local beach. A "tea walk" is something my good friend Jen came up with. Put your tea (or coffee) in an open mug, like a regular mug you'd use in your house, *not* a travel mug. With an open mug, you're forced to walk more slowly. You notice things you wouldn't ordinarily notice. I love the slow, meditative walk through my neighbourhood, and I love ending at the beach where I can breathe in the fresh marine air and let the sounds of the waves and the birds wash over me.

EMDR

The first time I did an EMDR (Eye Movement Desensitization and Reprocessing) session, it was on the recommendation of a good friend who had dealt with her fair share of trauma. I was certainly no stranger to talk therapy (also known as cognitive behavioural therapy, or CBT), but EMDR was a different animal. This was more of a somatic (mind-body) therapy, similar in a sense to breathwork. EMDR is about tapping into our subconscious to process and release old feelings, traumas and memories that have been trapped in our body for who knows how long.

When I first heard about EMDR from my friend Jordan, I was

pretty reluctant to try it myself. It sounded like it had worked well for her, but it also sounded like it would be super uncomfortable and difficult work to do. Knowing that I had a lot of stuff that needed processing and releasing, I eventually relented and gave EMDR a try. Luckily, Jordan had referred me to a very skilled therapist named Ellen, and I was definitely in good hands.

My EMDR sessions went very deep indeed. Sometimes, it wasn't even apparent what was being released or how the different pieces connected. The subconscious works in mysterious ways and holds on to connections that don't necessarily make sense to us when viewed through our conscious mind. I often needed some time after a session to fully process everything that had come up, and needed to be prepared for emotions to unexpectedly rise to the surface in the days following a session.

Here's what my sessions looked like. Ellen would direct me to:

- Close down my eyes.
- Tune into my breath.
- Breathe into the belly to calm the nervous system and get out of fight or flight mode.
- Tune into the observer part of the mind, instead of the experienced or judgmental parts.
- Choose a particular traumatic experience to use as the entry point (mine was usually the car accident concussion memory).
- Voice what I was envisioning and thinking about the car accident.

- Ellen would walk me through my detailed memories of the experience and different pieces of it.
- Sometimes we would explore what feelings or emotions were associated with the memories. Fear, guilt, anger, rage?
- Observe where in my body I felt the emotion lived. For me, it was often my chest or throat.
- Sometimes we would do other visualizations around a particular memory. Ellen might ask me what colour the feeling was and what shape. Is it smooth, round, jagged?
- Hold the feeling, breathe into it.
- Then, upon her signal, I would open my eyes and watch Ellen's finger as she moved it back and forth across my field of vision (doing the side-to-side eye movement is apparently what activates both hemispheres of the brain and helps the subconscious release the trapped energy and emotion).
- The last piece of the session was to compare how much emotional charge the memory had, as compared with how much charge it had before we had done the release. Almost invariably, the memory, feeling or statement we were working with held less of an emotional charge in my body after we had done the releasing.

I first learned about EMDR over a decade ago and, happily, it seems to be catching on more and more in recent years, along with many other somatic practices and therapies. As I mentioned above, I found

EMDR work to be confronting and not for the faint of heart, but in my mind, it's well worth the effort.

I think it's amazing that by tuning into my body and going deep for a shorter amount of time, I can release a bunch of traumas and carry on my way. Endless hours of talking, analyzing, and ruminating over past hurts, mistakes, and regrets no longer required? *Sign me up!*

I now realize that part of why this worked for me was that I went into it with a curious mind. Or at least curious enough to drown years of perfected sarcasm and aggressive self-judgment. Curiosity hasn't killed this Kat. However, on multiple occasions, it has most definitely saved it.

CHAPTER SIX
CONFETTI

In the early days of my separation, I found myself in a state that was eerily similar to my regular life, but it was also a "bizarro" world as I was traversing new terrain. I was going to work and pretending that all was well in my life. Meanwhile, I was an emotional wreck who was on the verge of tears most of the time. I cried myself to sleep often. I tried to tell myself that all was not lost. After all, I still have my beautiful daughter. Right? Well, partially right. I got to have her half the time, and my ex had her the other half. No big deal, right? *Wrong.* It was like losing a limb or holding my breath for a week at a time. I hated it. I was like a fish out of water.

One day, I was travelling back home from an out-of-town hearing. The case had wrapped up earlier than expected, giving me a rare early escape. The second I was able to switch off work mode, reality mode hit *hard*. It would make more sense to call it sad/raw/real life/ unstable/fragile mode. My marriage was over, and I was facing one of my first big stretches of time without my daughter.

I sped toward home, which, at that particular moment, was my friend's basement suite. My husband and I were doing something that I learned was called a nesting arrangement—in other words, my daughter stayed put in the house, and we rotated in and out every other week. When I was at the house with my daughter, my husband stayed with his mom, who lived a few minutes from our house. My family was off-island, so that wasn't possible for me, and as a consequence, I was homeless every other week, imposing on different friends and staying in their spare rooms.

After a few minutes or so of being on the road, reality set in that I would not be going home to my sweet girl when I got back into town. She'd be at home with her dad, and I would be in the suburban basement suite. One of the reasons I almost stayed in my marriage was to avoid this very situation. I couldn't even imagine seeing my daughter only half the time. I felt like my heart had been ripped from my chest.

Why was I in a hurry to find myself alone in a quiet space, devoid of the love and family I thought I was building? Everything was crumbling: all the things I thought my life was building toward, my carefully assembled house of cards, had fallen in spectacular bloody fashion.

Tears streamed down my face and filled my eyes until I couldn't see the road, forcing me to pull off the highway before I wrapped my car around a tree. I threw the car into park, and when my eyes regained focus, I Google-mapped my way to the Calico Cat.

I'd been told about it by some friends. Calico Cat was a tea house and restaurant which offered the bonus of someone reading your tea leaves. I had been meaning to make it there for months, but on that particular day, I was very much in need of a reading. It felt fortuitous that the tea house was on my route home from the court hearing.

Get it together, Kat!

I wiped my tears away with a car Kleenex. Cake would make it better, I decided. It sure as hell couldn't make it worse! So I went into the charming old heritage home that was now the tea house, hoping my failure, despair, and desperation didn't show.

I asked the hostess about getting a tea leaf reading.

She looked at me apologetically. "We're really busy this afternoon, hon, and I think the tea reader is fully booked today . . . but take a seat, and we'll see what we can do."

I found myself a table by a window and ordered a slice of carrot cake and a cup of tea. I distracted myself by checking my work emails and practised taking long, calming breaths between my bites and sips.

The hostess eventually came over to let me know there'd be no reading. "I'm sorry, hon. We're not going to be able to fit you in this afternoon."

"Okay, no problem. Thank you for trying." I nodded, trying my best not to dissolve right then and there.

I paid my bill, walked to the parking lot, got in my car, and cried.

Loudly. It was the middle of summer, and the car was probably over 100 degrees Fahrenheit, but I kept the windows up so no one would hear my pathetic wailing.

Pathetic. This was exactly where I deserved to be—bawling my eyes out while burning up in an oven of my own making.

Eventually, sanity and air conditioning brought me back to the problem at hand. I needed some guidance, and I needed a Plan B. Then it clicked.

Meredith and Alexandra!

I picked up my phone, got on Google, and found their booking website. Meredith and Alexandra were two intuitives who were also both moms and both worked in the finance industry. I had followed them on social media for a while and felt a bit of a kinship with them; they were corporate types and also spiritual girlies, like me. Alexandra was fully booked, but Meredith had a single opening in her schedule for Friday afternoon, just two days from then. I booked in for an intuitive reading and immediately felt a little better.

If the Universe, God, Spirit, or Source were really looking out for me, then this was one of the moments when I felt it. For whatever reason, the tea reading wasn't meant to work out, but I had scored an appointment with Meredith, and I trusted (i.e., desperately hoped) that I would get some of the guidance I badly needed during that reading.

In Shambles

Friday afternoon couldn't come fast enough. I sat in my friend's

Fig. 1. THE CHAKRAS (top to bottom):

CROWN Chakra (White or Purple) | Sahasrara | Spirituality, connection to the divine

THIRD EYE Chakra (Indigo) | Ajna | Intuition, foresight, wisdom, perception

THROAT Chakra (Blue) | Vishuddha | Expression, communication, authenticity

HEART Chakra (Green) | Anahata | Love, self-love, acceptance

SOLAR PLEXUS Chakra (Yellow) | Manipura | Power, self-esteem, confidence

SACRAL Chakra (Orange) | Svadhisthana | Creativity, pleasure, sexuality

ROOT Chakra (Red) | Muladhara | Security, safety, stability

basement suite and fired up my laptop to log in for my Zoom call with Meredith. It felt a little weird doing an intuitive reading on a video call, but I figured what the hell. I mean, I had done my oracle card pull with Kyla over Zoom, and that whole thing felt bang-on.

Meredith came online, and we chatted about how funny it was that a lawyer and a finance industry professional were sitting on Zoom together for an intuitive reading. I wonder if that was part of what made me feel safe with her? Her feet were on the ground, she had a regular day job, and she also did this.

Meredith explained that she would be doing an energy reading and that it would be in the order of the chakras. We started at the crown. "Spirit is very present," Meredith said. When she spoke about spirit, she explained that it could mean anyone from my spirit team—my spirit guides, my guardian angels, my ancestors, etc. "Your team is close by and wants to work with you. The crown chakra is at the top of your head and is your closest connection to spirit. When it's open, you can receive more from the Universe/spirit. They want you to know that they're here, and they're very eager to work with you. They are so glad you are finally showing up. They're showing me a beautiful, strong, glowing beam of pearly white light, extending up from your crown chakra towards the sky and towards the Spirit realm. They have a lot of help they want to provide. And they want you to remember that it's a two-way street: You can communicate with them, just as they will communicate with you. Ask them for help, ask for guidance. They want to support you."

After Meredith finished telling me about the energy of my crown chakra, we worked our way down to the third eye, the throat, and then to the heart chakra. "There is a lot of dense energy around your heart. A lot of hurt and trauma. Wounds. Injuries that are being carried in your heart. And not just from this lifetime. You're carrying the weight of traumas experienced by others in your female lineage." *Fabulous. As if I don't have enough of my own shit to deal with.*

"You need to do a lot of heart healing." *Do I ever*, I thought to myself.

"You have a daughter, right?" Meredith asked. I had NOT mentioned my daughter in any of our chit-chat before the reading. "Ah, I do actually, yes," I said quietly. I shouldn't have been surprised that she knew that, but somehow I was. "You have an opportunity to do this healing so that your daughter doesn't have to continue carrying this weight and learn these lessons in her lifetime."

We moved down to the solar plexus chakra. Meredith said that she was being shown an image of a wilted flower, trampled and unwell. "From your heart chakra to your solar plexus chakra is debilitated. Your solar plexus is where your personal power and confidence reside, and I can see that yours is in shambles."

Yep. Shambles described exactly how I was feeling right about then.

"You need to heal your heart and take back your power."

Naturally, I was in tears within moments. With the impending divorce and being separated from my daughter, the words coming from Meredith felt spot-on about the wounds I had suffered. This time, the tears felt more therapeutic than desperate, though. That was new.

Take back my power? Easier said than done.

I was too busy feeling like the weakest woman on earth at that moment.

As if reading my thoughts (*hah*), Meredith said, "You *can* do that. You can take it back. And if you do that, you'll be replanting the soil around this little flower, and it'll come back to life and bloom again and be so vibrant and stand so tall and strong. It will be so noticeable to everyone around you. Spirit wants you to know how big you're going to bloom, and how brightly you're going to shine again."

Hold up. "Did you know my daughter's name is Lily?" I asked.

"Your daughter's name is Lily?!" She gasped, letting the imagery and context register with the messages she had received. "I just got chills all over!"

That was when I was all in. So we went deeper. This is where shit gets weirder.

Meredith described images she'd been shown by my guides and angels. "You have all this pain and trauma, but it's not all yours. Some of it comes from your ancestral line."

I'd never heard of the **Akashic Records** before. Meredith informed me that each person (or more specifically, each soul) has a set of Akashic Records, where all of the information about our soul's past and future lives is stored. I tried to keep my mind open. "Most people's Akashic Records rooms look kind of like a library—books on the walls, that sort of thing," she said. "I've never seen one like yours. Yours is full of green rolling hills and blue sky. It's a serene, beautiful nature scene."

"So when I went into your Akashic Records, they kept saying 'fair maiden' and showing me a medieval woman in one of those tall, fancy hats. This cycle you're breaking . . . it goes back through your lineage, through the multiple lifetimes in which your soul has suffered trauma in romantic relationships. They're showing me the fair maiden for a reason, so I think this was your soul's first incarnation, or at least when these traumas began to take root. In that lifetime, for instance, you were mistreated and silenced by the man in your life who was supposed to protect you.

"They're also showing me an image of you at the starting block of a race or marathon. You know, like where the streets are lined with fans, cheering on the runners, but it's all your ancestors, spirit guides, angels, and supporters from the spirit realm. They are all there cheering you on, they're so supportive, so present, ready to root for you. They're saying, 'We know you can do this. You were meant for this. This is what we've been planning for.'"

Meredith also explained to me the concept of **soul contracts**. Soul contracts are contracts that your soul makes with other souls in the spirit world for what lessons you are meant to learn and experiences you're meant to have in this upcoming lifetime. It is the idea that, to some degree, all of the major events and relationships in our lives are preplanned. "You didn't do anything wrong," she reassured me.

"Your soul and his soul entered into a contract before this lifetime, and you were both meant to have that relationship, so that your soul could have those experiences and the opportunity to do this healing." Wow. I had convinced myself that I had chosen the wrong person to marry and build a life with. I was so mad I had gotten myself into that position and then had this disastrous experience. I had convinced myself it was *my* fault.

"You can do this," Meredith repeated. "You can choose to do this healing in this lifetime, if you want to. If you do, you will be breaking a cycle and helping to heal the traumas experienced by those who came before you."

"Okay, but how am I supposed to do all of this?" I asked, overcome by the mammoth nature of the task now before me.

Meredith recommended oracle cards (for communication with Spirit) and meditation (for heart healing). She was pleasantly surprised to hear that I had tried both already. She recommended guided meditations for heart healing, as well as silent sittings. "It doesn't have to be difficult or complicated or fancy," she said. "Just get really quiet and listen . . . Listen for what you hear, for what messages come through. I'm talking five to seven minutes to start; it doesn't have to be long."

It was, I realized, a lot like listening to my intuition. Just by getting still and listening, I could start to heal the intense pain and shame I had been feeling. This, in and of itself, felt like a bit of a relief.

Meredith described the concept of **breadcrumbs**. "Keep an eye out for the breadcrumbs that Spirit drops in your path. Follow them. It might be a book, a course, or a particular teacher. Something that grabs your interest. Follow that thread when you come across it. It will help lead you on this healing path." She also told me to keep my eye out for angel numbers and spirit animals. It sounds crazy, but I started seeing 1234 everywhere after the Meredith reading.

None of what she described to me could be considered a rational process, which my rational lawyer brain was admittedly struggling with. In my thinking mind, it was obvious to me that if something wasn't rational, it was therefore *irrational*. But this guidance from Meredith didn't feel irrational. I wasn't being asked to ignore or throw out the rational parts of my brain or the logic or truth I otherwise believed and trusted. I was, however, being asked to make space, make room for something outside of traditional logic. Instead of only believing that truth comes from logic and the mind, I came to understand that truth can also be intuitive, and it can come from the heart. It was not an either/or type situation . . . it was *AND*.

The explanations Meredith gave me and the information about soul contracts gave me so much comfort. It was so much better than thinking, "WTF is wrong with me?!" It gave more context for why I was perhaps going through what I was going through—why my life looked so different from so many others' lives. I had tons of friends in happy marriages, living the kind of life I wished I had. After my reading with Meredith, I was able to stop torturing myself by making direct comparisons to others around me. I came to understand that my path was different, and I was destined to have my own set of experiences and lessons that my soul had apparently chosen to have in this lifetime.

◇◇

MANTRA #5:

I need to heal my heart

and take back my power.

◇◇

More Spiritual Words

My education in all things spiritual was going pretty deep. This is a good time to share some more definitions so that we're all on the same page.

Intuition

Everyone has it, but not everyone uses it.

Remember when I said that one of the sources of guidance and wisdom is ourselves? Well, intuition is that source, baby. There is so much magic that already exists inside you. How exciting is that?!

We've all heard of "women's intuition" and "gut feelings." Most of us have no idea how to use or tap into our intuition. Some of us do it without trying, and to others, it's rather elusive or tricky to tap into. In a way, intuition is everywhere and nowhere all at the same time.

I think of intuition as little pieces of **invisible confetti** floating down around us all the time. Much of the time, when we are going about our daily lives and caught up in the busyness of our jobs, friends, kids, spouses, activities, chores, etc, etc, we aren't as likely to notice the little messages that may be within our grasp. But, when we slow down and get quiet—when we start to deliberately look and listen for these pieces of confetti—*that's* when we start to really see them and hear what they have to tell us. It's harder to do this when we are speed-walking from one appointment to the next. It's easier when we sit down on the park bench, and rest for a minute . . . That's when the goods will fall right into your lap.

Types of Intuitive Readers

Just about everyone would admit to having their fortune read for fun at a county fair or generally just for a laugh. But how many would also admit they had an unspoken wish that the reading would turn out to be true? That it hit so much closer to home than they ever expected?

The terms **psychics, mediums, intuitives, and future tellers** are all titles that have slightly different meanings and connotations. I figured that if *I* needed these titles and categories "demystified" (*ha ha, get it?*), then you might too. I decided to consult my two favourite intuitive experts—Meredith and Alexandra—and get the lowdown.

Basically, anyone doing work in this area is going to be an intuitive of some sort. Intuitives are experts at tapping into their intuition to receive messages from Spirit, Source, the Universe, their subconscious, or even loved ones who have crossed over, guides, or angels.

So why do some intuitives call themselves a psychic as opposed to a fortune teller, a medium or an energy reader? Terminology is often based on the person's specialty (intuitives can have different specialties, often based on the different ways they tap into their intuition) and their audience or situation.

As Meredith explained, it's most useful to adjust the labels used to speak in terms of what people can understand and accept in the moment. "When someone asks me what I do, and I say 'energy healings' and 'I work with energy,' they think electricity and aren't sure what the heck I'm talking about. So in those instances, it's easier to tell people I do 'psychic work' because that's a term they've heard before. By contrast, when talking to a bunch of fellow intuitives, for example, it's probably easier (and necessary) to be more precise about what kind of intuitive you are and what special skill it is that you tap into."

Mediums: When someone is working as a medium, they are channelling or communicating directly with someone on the "other side," i.e., in the spirit realm. This could be a deceased friend or relative, or it could be a member of your spirit team, like a spirit guide or a guardian angel. Working with a medium is a way to hear directly from someone, but of course, when you sit down for a session with a medium, the medium can't control who shows up from the spirit realm and who doesn't, so you will want to temper your hopes and expectations accordingly.

Psychics: This is the term that seems to get used most often, both in day-to-day conversation and Hollywood depictions of people who do intuitive work. The classic image that most people think of when they hear the word *psychic* is a fortune teller sitting at a table, peering over a crystal ball and seeing or predicting someone's future. Calling someone a psychic is an easy shorthand, but also an overused term. If you're thinking of someone who can see the future (aka *future-telling* or *fortune-telling*), you're probably thinking of a psychic or *clairvoyant*—a term I talk about more below.

I learned from Alexandra and Meredith that it's important to acknowledge that while a future teller may be able to tell you what they see for your future, it doesn't mean that is exactly how things are going to play out.

We all have divine free will. We can say yes or no to the options life presents to us. There are many, many routes your life could take, and a psychic will tell you about the version that Spirit is showing them, a version that is completely accessible to you. But it's also entirely optional for you. Meredith and Alexandra use the analogy of a bunch of train tracks that intersect with each other and go in all different directions. There are many possible routes you could take as a human being with free will. As you go through your life, making certain decisions about things, some tracks close off because you're not pursuing those options; meanwhile, the track you're on continues to be laid out before you, leading to your ultimate destination. Like with divine timing, some routes might be more like detours, leading back to a track that you initially avoided. When that happens, it's because there was an important lesson there for your soul to learn or a meaningful experience you needed to have.

Clairvoyants and other *clairs*: Most people think of clairvoyants as synonymous with psychics, but did you know there are other *clairs*, too? The *four clairs* are considered the most common modes of receiving intuitive messages.

1. **Clairaudience (hearing a message)**
2. **Clairvoyance (seeing a message)**
3. **Clairsentience (feeling a message)**
4. **Claircognizance (just knowing the message)**

I've come to learn that most of us are naturally strong in one or two of the clairs. We often just don't realize it. Our intuition and our intuitive gifts are something most of us have taken for granted or outright ignored.

When struggling with a big decision, such as "*Should I move cities?*" or "*Should I break up with this person?*", the logic-driven lawyer in me would previously have been more likely to write out a pros-and-cons list than to sit quietly and "feel into" what path is the right path for me.

Skilled intuitives have done the work and developed their ability to tap into all four clairs. Here's a little bit about each of them:

Clairaudience:. Clairaudience is when you hear a message in your mind. It often pops in as a short phrase or word. It could be something like "not yet" or "cross the street." Clairaudient messages often come in quietly and quickly, so the trick to developing this clair is to practise getting still and quiet enough to be able to hear these messages.

It might sound like someone else's voice, or it might sound like yours, but the voice you hear will be a calm, even tone. (Note that this is unlike voices that a person might hear if they are struggling with certain psychological conditions. If you are experiencing a mental health challenge, seek the help of a skilled medical professional.)

Clairvoyance: Clairvoyant messages arrive as an image or a scene in your mind. They could be literal (like seeing yourself running into an old friend on the street, and then later, actually running into that old friend), or they could be metaphorical (like seeing an image of someone lost in the woods, or carrying a heavy load). I'm also told that there are ways to strengthen this muscle. One exercise to try is attempting to guess an image or number from a deck of cards. Shuffle the deck, choose a card, and then close your eyes and wait to see if any images or numbers pop into your mind, seemingly out of the blue.

Clairsentience: A clairsentient message comes through as a physical sensation or feeling of some kind. Gut feelings fall into this category, as would the unspoken but palpable feeling you may get when the energy in a room suddenly shifts.

One of the coolest clairsentient sensations I have experienced myself of late is getting a chill or a shudder when something momentous (but usually subtle) is happening, like when I've had a significant personal realization, or gotten an idea for a poem or some such.

A friend of mine gets what she calls "truth chills" while she is in sessions with her clients and feels that something they've said is so bang-on, authentic, or a holy-hell-yes kind of thing. Others describe having an itchy throat or needing to clear their throat a lot when they, or someone they are with, is having trouble expressing their truth. It may indicate their throat chakra is closed off.

To practise honing this clair, try committing to a week of jotting down the times when one of these feelings or sensations comes through (even if it's just in the notes app on your phone). Note what the physical sensation was, and what was happening when it arrived. You might start to notice a pattern developing and realize you have a special awareness or talent for detecting something unseen.

Claircognizance: This is the feeling of "just knowing" something. Somehow, out of nowhere, you just know what you need to do, or you just know what the outcome will be. When I bought my first home, it was one of the first times that I had a knowing, a feeling that I now think of as claircognizance. I didn't have the vocabulary to describe it at the time. I just knew that this place needed to be my new home. A lot of people get similar feelings when house hunting, dating, choosing their bridal gown, naming their baby, creating a business, and more. Personally, I think my strongest intuitive sense is claircognizance. Funnily enough, I've had it assist me the two times

I've bought real estate, which is pretty awesome, because it meant that I went into both of those purchases with an odd, unwavering confidence that this was the condo/house for me. I think it's interesting that a logical, thoughtful lawyer like me can also have a decisive streak that, at times, propels me to do things. I'm not being impulsive or careless, but I am listening inward. And things tend to work out very well when I do.

Tapping into your clairs: Just about everyone experiences intuition or gut feelings that feel as if they're pointing down a path of some sort. Many in the woo community will tell you that's your clair abilities trying to help you. Do you feel like you're someone who ignores and overrules an intense gut feeling that doesn't necessarily make sense and seems to have arrived out of nowhere? One way to hone your claircognizance is to silently ask your intuitive self to bring you the answer and see what happens the next time you're trying to figure something out and your logical brain is having a tough time.

Spirit Guides

As I mentioned above, spirit guides are said to be souls who have completed all their lessons and are dedicated to guiding other souls through their life's challenges. Here's some more information about different types of Spirit Guides:

Archangels: Considered the leaders in the angel world, each archangel has a specialty, and they are all considered to have a powerful, large energy imprint. They can work with countless human beings at a time. So if you are in need of some specific help, ask for one of the archangels to visit you and assist with what you're facing. You can do this before bed, or during meditation, or really whenever.

Archangel Raphael is a popular one to call on, as his specialty is healing. But the others have lots to offer, too. Here are a few more archangels you might want to call on and their respective specialties: Ariel (connection to earth), Chamuel (nurturer, love, and self-love), Gabriel (messenger), Michael (he's the leader of the pack, and can apparently direct you to the angel who can help you best), Uriel (transformation, truth, light and wisdom) and Zadkiel (forgiveness and compassion) have lots to offer too.

Guardian Angels: Everyone is said to have a guardian angel who was assigned to them at birth (unlike archangels, who are available to help everyone). Your guardian angel helps you throughout your lifetime, and they are yours exclusively! Call on your guardian angel anytime you need assistance, and get ready to receive their unconditional, non-denominational love.

Your guardian angel's mission is to guide, protect, and serve you while helping you along your spiritual path—a spiritual concierge, if you will, always on-call. Like other spirit guides, your guardian angel won't insert itself in your life without your free will . . . unless, of course, there's a life-threatening situation that crops up before it is your time to leave your earthly body. Your angels are here to help—you just have to ask them.

"Regular" Angels / Angel Numbers: All angels (whether *arch*, *guardian,* or just a run-of-the-mill spiritual being in the angelic hierarchy) can communicate messages, provide comfort and protection, and give you helpful soul guidance.

One way that I like to remember that angels are around me and that my spirit guides are communicating with me is when I see angel numbers. The quintessential angel number is 11:11, so if you keep noticing 11:11, or 12:12 or 5:55 (or whatever) on the clock (or on receipts, licence plates, etc), know your angels are nearby and are looking over you. Angel numbers can be any pattern or repetition of numbers that you notice yourself seeing a bunch of times in a row. There was a point in time when I started to see 12:34 all over the place. I didn't know what to make of it, and hadn't heard of angel numbers before, but when I mentioned it to a friend, she Googled "angel number 1234" and sent me the link . . . let's just say the message associated with 1234 was spot-on for where I was at, and was such a reassuring communication to receive.

Ancestors: Ancestral spirit guides are connected to you through genetic memory. They can support you in repairing ancestral traumas and genetic scarring that have persisted through the generations in your lineage. This work repairs that of the past, bringing it forward into the present, and perpetuating the repair through the future.

Spirit Animals: The term descends from Indigenous cultures of North America and around the world, and it is important to be mindful of this and not to unwittingly replicate or appropriate the traditional animal imagery from totem poles or pictographs. That being said, it is not cultural appropriation to want to connect with your own spirit animal.

A spirit animal can be an invaluable and incredibly unique guide who can help you on your journey. You can have more than one spirit animal, or you can have a single spirit animal who has been with you your whole life. I have certain spirit animals who make cameo appearances during certain periods in my life, or for a particular purpose.

Much like other spirit guides, spirit animals will start to show themselves to you in subtle but meaningful ways. If you begin to notice an animal appearing in your dreams or when you meditate, take note! That could be your spirit animal coming to introduce themself. I was on a trip once with a girlfriend, and she kept seeing owls *everywhere*—at our Airbnb, in shops, on labels of wine bottles, you name it. Turned out, the owl had special meaning to her mom (who was going through a difficult time, health-wise), and the owl's association with being a fierce protector with deep wisdom was particularly fitting for their circumstances at the time.

CHAPTER SEVEN
Breadcrumbs

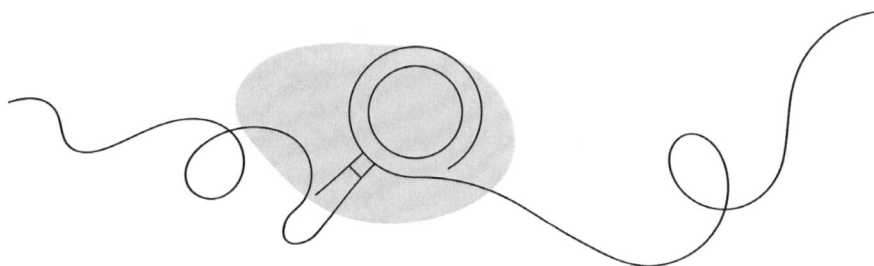

The first breadcrumb that got dropped in my path following my energy reading with Meredith was an email from Kyla. She and I weren't in touch as regularly after she stopped doing personal training, but we texted occasionally, and I was still on her email list. Every so often, typically when I was procrastinating on another task, I'd browse my junk email folder, and on that particular day in late August, I stumbled upon Kyla's latest newsletter. One of the events she mentioned was a breathwork retreat in Costa Rica that she was going to be co-hosting over the New Year.

My heart skipped a beat. I had been to Costa Rica once before, with Rosie (and loved it). I knew and trusted Kyla. And I needed some soul healing in a major way. And since breathwork seemed to be some kind of trauma healing modality (based on what I could glean from Kyla's social media posts), this retreat looked right up my street. Kyla's email blast said there were three spaces left.

The Universe spoke, and I listened. I texted Kyla later that day to tell her I was interested, and she immediately wrote back, excitedly telling me how amazing the retreat was going to be and how great her co-facilitators (a couple of guys named Cam and Ryan) were. She put me in touch with Cam, who was doing intake interviews with everyone who applied for the retreat. I learned that they were creating a container of people, and they wanted to ensure the personalities, intentions, and vibes of all the participants were aligned before accepting someone into the retreat.

I had never been in a "container" before. But I figured, yeah, if I'm going to be in a metaphorical Tupperware with these people for seven days in a foreign country, an intro call was probably a good idea before I signed on.

Before my call with Cam, I had looked at all the promo material they had posted about the retreat to see what I was getting myself into. It looked like it was going to be quite the experience—there would be some yoga, lots of breathwork (again, I still had no real idea what that meant), and a bunch of outdoor adventures—images of people dancing in jungles, surfing, jumping off waterfalls, that sort of thing.

Cam didn't present as the typical *Om Shanti* yogi spiritual type that I had stereotyped in my head. Cam had a shaved head, lots of tattoos, and even more muscles. His energy and enthusiasm were infectious, and even though there was a "bro" vibe about him, it was clear that there was more to him than that. I was intrigued. Plus, Kyla had vouched for him, and that counted for a lot in my books.

We did the intake meeting, and at the end of our chat, Cam asked me if I had any questions. "You're not going to make me jump off a waterfall or anything, are you?!" I asked, only half jokingly. Cam winked, smiled, and said, "Look, Kat, no one's going to make you do anything."

Oh great. There would be waterfall jumping. At least I knew I had the option of opting out.

Wine Club

I remember fessing up to my upcoming Costa Rica adventure at Wine Club (a casual get-together with friends that met every few weeks). We were a group of four female professionals: a lawyer (me), an accountant, a marketing executive, and a biologist. They were not particularly woo.

So there we were, sitting around in one of their living rooms, drinking a bunch of wine and eating charcuterie, talking about what our plans were over the upcoming winter holidays. I blurted out, "I'm going on a breathwork retreat to Costa Rica!" I took a big gulp of wine and prepared myself for potential backlash.

"What exactly is a breathwork retreat?" asked one friend.

"And why is it in Costa Rica?" asked another.

I tried to explain. "It's more of a yoga, meditation, *and* breathwork retreat . . ." I struggled to find the right words, mostly because I didn't really know what it was all about myself.

One friend looked concerned. "You're not going to do Ayahuasca or any of those crazy hallucinogenic drugs in some hut in the jungle, are you?"

"Aya what?" I had never even heard of Ayahuasca at the time. There certainly was no aya-whatever at the retreat.

I could tell they wanted to support me, but were skeptical—maybe worried is a better word—about me going off to the jungles of Costa Rica to do anything.

I didn't want to divulge much more for fear of being seen as a woo-woo weirdo, and so I grew quiet.

Luckily, one of them got excited about the travel side of things, and we all fell into a conversation about travel, future adventures, and bucket lists, leaving all things woo in the rearview and me wishing that I could be as passionate about the topic in person as I was at heart.

Trust Falls in Costa Rica

Cam and Kyla informed me that the retreat was not the kind of container where there would be any kind of peer pressure. I reminded myself that I trusted Kyla. She trusted Cam. And that meant everything would be alright.

The first night of the retreat was more woo than I had ever been immersed in before. The other folks who were there were an interesting mix of people. There were a couple of basic-looking women like me, some emo dudes, a few spiritual bros (a category I truly didn't realize existed until I had met Cam), and a couple embodied hippie types spouting all the lingo, and sporting the flowy wardrobe to go along with it.

That night, we were all asked to set some intentions and then write words down on pieces of paper that represented things we were ready to release. Then we burned the paper, drank some cacao (ceremonial, super-high-quality hot chocolate intended to open the heart), partnered up and put our hands on each other's hearts, and then did a breathing/connection exercise. I connected with a group of strangers that night in an oddly comforting and non-weirdly intimate way.

We also did some group exercises, including one that helped us tune into our **Sacred Yes** and our **Sacred No**. The idea behind these concepts is that whatever choice you are making or activity you are engaging in should feel fully aligned for you. We practiced checking in with ourselves, exercising our Sacred No, and respecting when something was a No for someone else in the group. I deeply appreciated and respected the facilitator team's focus on this. I knew that if jumping off the waterfall was truly a Sacred No for me, that decision would be respected by the group.

As we were saying our goodnights, Cam informed us that the next morning would be our waterfall field trip. Shit. We were really going to do this. We woke up before dawn and boarded our mini-bus to traverse the bumpy dirt roads of rural Costa Rica. I was sitting in the back corner of the bus, which felt fitting since I wanted to cocoon myself away and pretend like I wasn't about to either: (a) jump off a fucking waterfall, or (b) be the only person in the group who was too scared to jump off the fucking waterfall.

Being in the back corner of the bus meant I was sitting directly over the wheel well, and the bounces and bumps were nothing short of nasty. My tailbone was bruised for like two weeks after that. *Did I mention I cried the whole ride up? Sounds like quite the amazing vacay I'd taken myself on, huh?!*

About twenty minutes in, the woman sitting next to me, a mom from somewhere in the American Midwest, turned to me and gently asked if I wanted to chat. She must've seen my discomfort and felt bad for me. I couldn't even croak out an answer, so I just shook my head no. She waited a minute and then reached over and softly said, "Can I hold your hand?"

I nodded, took her outstretched hand, and mouthed the words "thank you" while tears streamed silently down my face. No judgment, no interrogation, no fanfare. Just a hand to hold when I needed it. (This is just one part of the magic that I have come to love about retreats and the people I meet at them.)

We parked at our destination, and I gingerly climbed off the bus, sliding my sunglasses over my eyes to cover my tear-stained face. Everyone else was chatty, and some people were clearly looking forward to this potential death jump.

The theory behind this excursion was explained to us by the facilitators with the acronym LEAP—Leading Experiences to Actualize

Potential. It means that when you do something momentous like this, and you do it with intention and forethought, it can be a catalyst for personal growth, fulfilment, and meaningful change.

As a group, we dropped into meditation (because I could do that now) and were asked to "feel into" two things—what we were letting go of, and what we were leaping into. The words that came through for me loud and clear were fear and trust. I was ready to let go of fear and ready to leap into trust. Having solidified our intentions, we were told that as we jumped, we should yell out the thing we were calling in. As a way of viscerally and symbolically immersing ourselves in the intention and truly embodying what it was that we were calling in.

Eventually, it was my turn to jump. I nervously shuffled my way along the wet rocks over to Ryan, the facilitator who was stationed at the top of the waterfall to talk us through the jump. I got to the jumping spot, and Ryan asked how I was feeling.

"Scared out of my fucking mind, Ryan, how are you?" I answered, trying not to look down.

He chuckled knowingly. I surely wasn't the first person to have a panic attack while staring down a potential near-death experience.

"What are your two words?" he asked.

"Fear, and trust," I laughed between chattering teeth. I was shaking. "Ironic, huh? Since I'm scared shitless to do this jump, and yet what I want to feel more of in my life is trust."

Ryan gently and oh-so-steadily talked me through my fears

(rational, irrational, and everything in between) about the jump I was about to take.

I had just watched eight other people do it safely, and Ryan and I talked through all the rational reasons why this was not a reckless, unsafe thing to do. There had been so much inner dialogue leading up to this, so many voices in my head (mostly fear-based) about what could happen to me and how badly I could injure myself if this jump went badly. Not to mention how mad and disappointed my parents would be if I hurt myself doing something stupid like this. Plus, I was a mom now, and I had my daughter to think about too.

Ryan led me through some deep breathing. I cried (of course). And, eventually, when I couldn't come up with any more reasons not to, I felt ready to jump. I felt calm. Most importantly, I felt brave. I was doing this jump for myself (and, by extension, for my daughter). I wanted to step away from some of my old patterns and relationships and embrace the next chapter of my life, as unknown and scary as that seemed at the time.

I stood up there for longer (much longer) than anyone else had, and no one said a thing. No one pushed me to hurry up. In this group, it was okay to take up space; it was okay to ask for what I needed, and take the time to feel truly ready until I was fully okay taking the next step on my terms.

Ryan counted me down. Three . . . two . . . one . . . And I jumped. Me. Lawyer Kat. Semi-Woo Kat. Safe and logical Kat. *I jumped!!* And I trusted. And I screamed all the way down.

I plunged into the water at the bottom, going under for what felt like twenty seconds but was probably only two. When I emerged and got my bearings, I heard a sound, but it was muffled. I shook my head to help get some of the water out of my ears, and that's when I realized what I was hearing. My fellow retreaters—friends whom I had known for less than a day—were all screaming, cheering, and clapping for me. I blinked the water out of my eyes until I could see Ryan, up there at the top, fist pumping and smiling ear to ear.

Cam swam over to me. "You did it, Kat! Proud of you, sister," he said. I swam with him to the water's edge, where one of the other retreaters extended his (very muscular) arm to help me out of the water and onto the rocks. (Seriously, who knew there were so many hot, fit men who were into spirituality and personal development?)

I was safe. My feet were on the ground again. And my spirit was soaring. I did it! I did it *and* I didn't die. In fact, I felt truly alive. If this was what growth felt like, I wanted more.

That retreat changed my life. And some of the people I met there have since become like family to me.

Deep Breaths in Mexico

In Costa Rica, I was taken to the edge and back, healed, loved, and shown how much more there is to this life than I ever realized.

I continued doing "the work" and eventually felt ready for the challenge and emotional surge of another breathwork retreat. Costa

Rica was a breathwork retreat, but as I learned in my next retreat, I had barely scratched the surface in Costa Rica. The next retreat I signed up for was in Mexico and was run by Kyla alone. My breathwork experiences had been getting deeper, but Mexico is where things went to a whole other level.

A little nugget of wisdom that I have since learned: Spirit/Universe/Source gives you what you need, not what you want, and it also sends you what you're able to handle at any particular time. So, in my situation, I must not have been truly ready to see the things I saw or receive the messages I received until I was lying on that beach in Mexico. And by the same token, even when something feels like a lot, when the experience is uncomfortable in the extreme, you can take heart in knowing that Spirit won't give you more than you can handle. This knowledge has gotten me through some dark nights, knowing that what's been thrown at me is perfectly on time and isn't going to drown me, even when it feels like it might.

Everything changed for me on that remote beach south of Tulum. We stayed in a protected bio-reserve area. It was a four-hour drive from Tulum, down a bumpy dirt road (luckily, my tailbone survived this time). The location was rustic and oh so beautiful. It was tropical and raw, not over-touristed like so many other parts of the country. We had a private beach all to ourselves, and the ocean was deliciously warm to swim in. Every afternoon during that seven-day retreat, we did Conscious Connected Breathwork (we'll use the acronym CCB for convenience) outdoors.

Breathwork took a while to grow on me. I stuck with it, trusting that it wasn't just going to be an easy, immediate "ah ha" moment (although I think it can be for some people; for me, it took me a while to truly sink into it).

I realize that going on a breathwork retreat sounds crazy to some people.

A sane person might ask, "Why do you have to travel to a foreign country just to breathe, Kat? Don't you already know how to breathe?"

To which Woo Kat might've replied, "Okay, yes, I know how to breathe. But not like that. *Nothing* like that."

Plus, this retreat was led by a "breathwork practitioner." When you hear that term or someone saying they've had a "breathwork journey," they are almost certainly talking about Conscious Connected Breathwork. Like just about everyone else on the planet, I'd done focused, deep breathing and box breathing from time to time. I'd also done mindful breathing during guided meditations and some other little techniques to help calm my nervous system down when necessary, but *whoa!* Those were nothing compared to this.

CCB involves a style of circular breathing, where you breathe only through your mouth, and remove the pause between the inhale and the exhale.

The idea is that when you breathe in this fashion for an extended period (thirty to sixty minutes, or more), the frontal cortex of your brain goes offline for a bit, your blood increases in alkalinity, and your body can experience feelings of tingling or tremors. The physiological changes from breathing in this intentional (conscious), circular (connected) way are temporary and not harmful to the body. And, most importantly, they put your body into a state where you bypass your rational thinking brain and tap into the subconscious much more easily and deeply.

Some retreats use substances to enhance the depth of the journey, but as you might have guessed, I was the kind of person who said no to drugs, whether the cool kids were doing them or not. I have a healthy fear of what could potentially go wrong. No peyote or Ayahuasca in a jungle hut for me! And that's okay, because CCB works without it.

With CCB, I felt safe and in control. I chose how slow or fast I wanted to go, and I could stop it if things became too overwhelming.

My first several experiences doing CCB mainly involved me having physical and emotional releases. Lots of them—crying, sobbing, and tremors. It was as if I had been stuck for as long as I could remember, filled with gunk that weighed me down and suffocated me, and with each breath, I was releasing said gunk from my system. Each day, I left those sessions feeling lighter than when I entered. I was clearing out old, trapped emotions that I had dutifully spent my lifetime stomping and stuffing down until then. A lifetime of telling myself to "play like it didn't hurt."

Plenty of people cry during breathwork (so I wasn't alone in that sense). But some people, on the other hand, seemed to be having an entirely different kind of breath journey. There was giggling, people who spoke of visions and spirit animals. One time, someone broke into song (I'm not even kidding).

After each breath journey, there was a sharing circle, where people had the option of sharing any insights or revelations they had, or really anything at all about their experience. Some folks shared about their joyful, lighthearted, good times.

My breathwork journeys became straight up CINEMATIC on that beach. If I hadn't had these experiences myself, I would probably think they were horseshit, or at the very least, exaggerated. I'm talking visions of spirit animals, some of whom delivered messages to me. Images of a phoenix rising from my chest while I lay there, arms outstretched, with flames rising up from the palms of both my hands.

Another thing that happens to me sometimes in a breath journey is that I feel taller. Like, I feel that my five-foot, six-inch body sprouted up to six feet. The longer I breathed in this way, the more space and room it felt like I had in my body. I felt expansive—open and free. *I know all of this may sound looney tunes, but put me on the stand and cross-examine me, and I'll stick to my story. This shit is real. At least it is for me.*

Even though there is a long history of substance-assisted psychotherapy, I didn't need psychedelics or hallucinogens to have these experiences. The medicine is the breath, and that is wild! I love the fact that one of the most powerful mechanisms for healing trauma uses something we already have right inside our own bodies.

Turning inward for insight and healing has become one of the biggest lessons and themes of my life. The effects can be profound.

Through CCB, I have experienced the physical release of trauma, pain, and emotions that my body had been holding onto for years or even decades. It was like ridding myself of a mask I hated or being set free from a cage I didn't even realize I was trapped in.

CCB is another one of those things that can be practised remotely (I do so regularly), and it can also be practised in-person in a group setting, or even one-on-one with a facilitator. I highly recommend doing breathwork journeys with a trained facilitator. You will want to work with someone knowledgeable in the kinds of things you might experience during a journey, someone skilled and tuned in to helping you process and release whatever is coming up for you.

The benefits of breathwork, broadly stated, typically include increased clarity and well-being. More specific benefits can range from enhanced immune function, lowered stress and lower blood pressure, to the lessening of anxiety and depression symptoms, as well as the processing and healing of trauma, PTSD, and grief. Researchers have started running studies involving CCB to determine its effectiveness in treating more run-of-the-mill ailments like chronic lower back pain. To me, that's a great sign that the established medical community is starting to take note of the benefits of CCB; hopefully, it will help legitimize and popularize breathwork practices even further.

During the Mexico retreat, I talked with people about their experiences with Ayahuasca and other plant medicines. Several of them said that a breathwork journey (i.e., CCB alone) would routinely take them as deep or deeper than any of the psychoactive substances. One of the pioneers of CCB, Stanislav Grof, developed his particular breathwork style (referred to as Holotropic Breath) as a way to replicate the effects of the psychedelic drug LSD, at a time when LSD was being rendered illegal and becoming inaccessible even for therapeutic uses.

Breath is literally the most accessible tool you have to tap into your body and your inner knowing, and it's about time we all learned how to use it to its full potential.

◇◇

MANTRA #6:
The things that will help me heal
are already inside of me.

◇◇

Plant Medicines and Psychedelics

I know many people who have taken one of the "plant medicines," such as psilocybin (magic mushroom) or Ayahuasca, and have had incredibly deep, spiritual experiences with plant medicine. Other people find success without them. Personally, I have had visions during breathwork that are wilder and more vivid than I ever expected possible *without* psychedelic substances.

And just as meditation and yoga have entered the mainstream, psychedelic-assisted therapy is quickly becoming more accepted in the medical and academic communities. There are therapy clinics that specialize in integrated psychotherapeutic approaches such as EMDR, somatic therapy, Deep Brain Reorienting (DBR), and mindfulness.

Vancouver Island University, for example, now offers a psychedelic-assisted therapy program that brings together doctors, nurses, elders and traditional practitioners, and incorporates both Western and Indigenous methodologies for healing and treatment. Nursing Professor Dr. Shannon Dames is quoted as saying, "In a psychotherapy realm, we primarily talk to people at the level of the mind, which may or may not impact people at the level of the body, where trauma resides. In psychedelic-assisted therapy, the nervous system moves into the background, enabling people to drop into their bodies. And it's in this place that the potential to tend to unhealed wounds and re-orient oneself to the world becomes possible."

Something tells me that the use of plant medicines and other psychedelics in conjunction with traditional Western methods for treating mental health issues is not as far around the corner as we may think it is.

Bite-Sized Breathwork Exercises

Here are some breathwork exercises you can try (note: these are not the same as doing a conscious connected breathwork journey—these are great little exercises that you can incorporate into your day-to-day regimen):

Box Breathing

*   ★ Inhale slowly and deeply through your nose for a count of four.
*   ★ Hold your breath for a count of four.
*   ★ Exhale your breath slowly out through your mouth for a count of four.
*   ★ Hold again for a count of four.
*   ★ Repeat.

Alternate Nostril Breathing

*   ★ Bring your right hand to your face, and use your thumb to close your right nostril.
*   ★ Inhale deeply through your left nostril, then close it with your ring finger, release your thumb, and exhale through your right nostril.
*   ★ Inhale through the right nostril, close it, and exhale through the left.
*   ★ That is one round. Repeat five to ten times.

Breath of Fire

*   ★ Start with a few normal breaths—take a few deep breaths in and out to centre yourself and prepare for the technique.
*   ★ Begin with gentle breaths, in a slow and steady rhythm,

focusing on equal inhales and exhales, pushing the belly button in and out with each breath.

★ Once you're comfortable with the pattern, gradually increase the speed of your inhalations and exhalations.

★ As you exhale, engage the core by contracting your abdominal muscles, pulling your belly button towards your spine.

★ Maintain equal breaths by inhaling and exhaling through the nose with equal force and duration, maintaining a consistent rhythm.

★ Continue for a set time. For newbies, it is best to start small. Begin with thirty seconds and gradually increase the duration as you become more comfortable, up to several minutes.

★ Return to normal breathing after the set time by gently transitioning back to a normal breathing pattern.

A Tale of Two Potlucks

Sometime after I was well into my woo journey, I was scheduled to attend two separate potlucks. One was an annual summer barbecue with my lawyer colleagues and friends, and the other was a potluck with my newfound spiritual retreat peeps.

At the spiritual peeps' potluck, we didn't do any spiritual activities or anything—no meditations, no chanting, no mind-altering substances. We just ate, talked, laughed, and shared stories. It was easy, fun, and intimate. I had three or four deep conversations that evening. The host showed us her new singing bowls. I made plans with one woman to go to the new Nordic spa in town. I left feeling very seen and very loved.

At the work potluck, we also ate, talked, and laughed. Most people were drinking (a lawyer party without alcohol is kind of like a swimming pool without water), and we also sang songs around a campfire, shot some pool, and played beer pong, but with water in the cups instead of beer (gotta hydrate once you hit a certain age). I reconnected with a couple of my work besties and we had long-overdue catch-up chats. I left feeling respected and connected.

I do not want to make it seem like I work with a bunch of vapid, superficial lawyer robots. Because I don't. I love the many generous, funny, sensitive, empathic, and kind individuals within my work community. That being said, there are some marked differences between the people in each of my two worlds.

Case in point: I was at the work potluck, sitting around a patio table with a handful of work peeps, when one of them asked, "Have I ever told you guys about the time I settled a lawsuit because of what my client's horoscope said?!" Everyone laughed. I mean, what kind of illogical, half-wit client would settle a lawsuit based on their horoscope instead of the sensible advice from their legal counsel?

The story, in a nutshell, was about a client who was extremely indecisive and wouldn't take her lawyer's advice, which was to accept the other side's settlement offer and conclude the lawsuit. According to my work friend, this particular client did not have a very good case, and the lawyer had tried reasoning with her on many occasions. They were at the courthouse about to start a two-week-long trial, which, in this day and age, costs tens of thousands of dollars to run (if not more); plus, judicial resources are scarce, so when a judge senses a dispute could be ripe for settlement, they will sometimes try to not-so-subtly nudge parties in that direction. The presiding judge did just that: They adjourned the hearing to essentially force the two sides to have one last go at settlement talks.

After some discussions on the courthouse steps, the lawyer (my colleague) took her client to a nearby café to grab a coffee and have a bit of a breather. Lawsuits can be traumatizing, frankly. They can turn you inside out to the point where you don't even listen to the legal professional you've hired to act in your best interests.

The lawyer and her client sat at their booth. There was a newspaper on the table in front of them. The lawyer leafed through the paper and came across the horoscope section. She read her own horoscope aloud, then asked her client what her sign was and read hers too. It read: *You are going to be faced with a difficult decision this week; seek advice from an older relative.* The lawyer (somewhat flippantly) asked her client, "Do you have any older relatives whom you might want to call for advice?"

The client tried calling her favourite aunt, but got no answer. Then she tried her grandmother, who did answer. The client told her the whole story, including the lawyer's advice to take the settlement offer, and asked her grandmother what she thought she should do.

"Sounds like you should listen to your lawyer, take the offer and be done with this whole mess, sweetie!" the wise elderly woman exclaimed. The client instructed her lawyer to accept the settlement offer, and the case was concluded that afternoon.

This anecdote was met with much gregarious laughter around the table of lawyers at the barbecue.

At the woo potluck, instead of laughter, I can guarantee that the horoscope court case resolution story would've been met with, "Aw, that makes so much sense. Good for her for listening to her inner guidance!" or, "Sounds like she needed a sign and the Universe gave her one! How amazing."

Sitting around the table with my law peeps, I didn't speak up one way or the other about the story. I didn't fly any spiritual flags or admit that I respected the client's decision to follow her gut. It felt like there was just too much of a divide between these two worlds. Mainstream and woo. Lawyer Kat and Woo Kat.

Yet again, I felt a deep divide between two realms of my existence. I wasn't yet brave enough to "out" myself to my lawyer friends, but the breadcrumbs were too compelling. I felt a magnetic pull to the spiritual path that I wasn't prepared to ignore.

CHAPTER EIGHT
EVERYTHING IS ENERGY

O ne of my favourite lessons I've learned so far is that "every-thing is energy." And I mean *everything*. Knowing this has been pretty foundational and extremely helpful when trying to make sense of it all.

Likely, the first time you heard this was in tenth-grade physics, where you were taught that everything on the planet (and beyond, for that matter) is made up of teensy-tiny vibrating particles of energy. The book or device you are reading this on is made up of vibrating energy particles. The chair you're sitting on is made up of vibrating energy particles. Same with the floor your cat is currently loafing on, the rocks on your favourite forest path, and the grass you love to step on with bare feet.

CHAPTER EIGHT

Most of us had a very tangible, literal upbringing. Everything in our lives is made up largely of what we can see, hear, taste, touch, and smell. By comparison, the spiritual world of energy and vibration can feel pretty far out there at times. It requires you to reserve your judgment, to trust, and to believe that there is more here than what we can see or hold.

My advice to you: keep an open mind and hang on for the ride. In case it resonates with you, the image that is coming to my mind right now as I write these words is how Ebenezer Scrooge in *A Christmas Carol* just had to touch the sleeve of the spirits he was visited by to lift off and fly with them across time and space.

I also love that scene toward the end of the movie where he's dancing around his bedroom, singing: "I don't know anything, I never did know anything. Now I know that I don't know, all on a Christmas morn." I have felt this same way after some of my meditations and breathwork journeys, and holy hell is it a powerful and liberating realization to have.

◇◇

MANTRA #7:

I don't know anything.

I never did know anything.

But now I know that I don't know!

◇◇

Vibrations (Good Vibes, Bad Vibes, and Everything in Between)

Vibrations. They're woven into the fabric of literally everything about us and everything around us. The law of vibration is considered one of the universal laws. This particular law states that everything that exists in our universe—whether seen or unseen—consists of energy and vibrates at a particular frequency.

At a microscopic level, everything around us is made up of tiny particles that are in constant motion, vibrating at a specific frequency. If you're on board with the idea that everything around us is made up of vibrational energy, then the next logical step is to realize that this also means you. YOU have a personal frequency and are energetically vibrating at a particular rate, depending on your physical, mental, and emotional states. The law of vibration tells us that our vibrational frequency can inform our lived experience.

Here's where things start to get really interesting: we can alter our own energetic vibration (i.e., raise our frequency) by changing the way we think, feel, act, etc. That means the "Good Vibrations" we've been singing about for so long (whether they be by The Beach Boys or by Marky Mark and the Funky Bunch—I don't judge), are real.

But that doesn't mean that it's all good vibes all the time. Nowadays, we are inundated with T-shirts, mugs, and journal covers that scream "Good Vibes Only!" Cute, right? Well, the older I've become, the less I like being told what to do, and the more of my inner wisdom

I've discovered, which means I sure as shit don't like being told I can only have good vibes. Sorry, but no.

ALL Vibes Welcome

I believe that in a world where everything is energy, all vibes should be welcome. No one is happy all the time, just as no one is sad all the time.

Have you ever heard of an Emotional Vibrational Frequency Chart? It maps different human emotions to specific vibrational frequencies, usually measured in Hertz (Hz). A well-known version of the chart was developed by Dr. David R. Hawkins in his book *Power vs. Force: The Hidden Determinants of Human Behavior*. The concept is that every emotion or state of consciousness has a measurable frequency. Positive emotions are said to vibrate at higher frequencies, and negative ones at lower frequencies. Shame and guilt are the lowest at 20 and 30 Hz, respectively. The highest are love, peace, and enlightenment, ranging from 500 Hz to 700+ Hz.

It's easy to see how the lower-vibration emotions can get a bad rap. It's not exactly fun to sit in feelings of fear, guilt, or shame, yet those are totally valid, necessary aspects of the human experience. Remember: without the dark, there can be no light. If everything was great all the time, that would become a pretty flat, one-dimensional experience, no? Maybe it's because I grew up in the Pacific Northwest and I'm used to experiencing different seasons, but it strikes me that waking up every single day to the same version of So-Cal sunshine would get a bit tedious after a while.

I think one of the big things I've struggled with on this front is when I see these people who *only* display love, gratitude, and optimism, no matter the day or circumstance. While there may be people who only see sunshine, I'm not one of them. That, to me, feels forced and artificial. If all you are, all the time, is love and light and positivity and rainbows, then amazing, BUT it's okay, and even expected, for all of us to have a tough moment or even a bad day from time to time.

While most of us can't (and don't need to) feel *#blessed* one hundred percent of the time, we also don't want to constantly live in the doldrums or exist only in the lower-vibration emotions. That wouldn't be so great either. So, what can we do when we want to vibrate at a higher frequency and embody the high-vibe emotions a bit more? The answer is: climb that ladder, rung by rung. If you're feeling low, don't force or "should" yourself into trying to feel joy just so you can eradicate the fear or sadness you might be feeling. You can't jump straight from despair to joy. The better approach is to reach for the next level up from where your current emotional state is.

So if I'm feeling pessimistic and irritated, I might try to gently nudge myself to see the hopefulness in a particular situation, or try looking at things a bit more optimistically and assume that things will work out for the best, not the worst. What I *don't* do is berate myself into feeling "joy, joy, JOY!!" (because, guess what, the berating part kind of hamstrings you from getting to the actual joy part). The Pollyanna approach has never worked for me, and I have my doubts that it works for anyone.

One of my favourite ways to shift my energy and raise my vibration is to *move* the energy—do something to move the energy and shift my energetic state.

This can look like a whole bunch of things, depending on the state I'm in, my current mood, and the tools and space currently available to me.

Sometimes, after a shitty day, it's a kitchen dance party set to "Shake It Off," or a five-minute breathwork practice to shake out the stuck, heavy energy that is dragging me down. Sometimes it's journaling, taking a walk in nature, letting myself cry it out, or going to an exercise class.

And sometimes, after a shitty marriage, screaming into the void can be helpful (I speak from experience). I've done this a couple of times in my car (windows up, of course), screaming so loud my throat hurt after. Yelling into a pillow is also a good way to do this, so that the neighbours don't call for a wellness check! Howling at the moon and screaming in the woods are things I haven't yet attempted, but I hear can be quite therapeutic.

If one wishes to be a little less dramatic about it, another of my favourites is to throw on Alanis Morissette's "You Oughta Know" and sing along like I did when I was fifteen years old. Anyone else with me?

Constructively moving the energy *doesn't* mean numbing out with substances and sitting on the couch binging Netflix . . . as tempting as I know that can be. We've all done it. But it won't come as a surprise when I tell you that avoiding or stuffing down the emotions, negative energy, whatever you want to call it, isn't an effective way of processing or moving through it. The feelings need to be *felt*.

Grounding is another excellent and super simple practice. Grounding just refers to putting your human body in contact with the earth. Go outside—walk on some grass, stick your toes in the sand. Or, hug a tree if that's your thing.

There are countless ways to shift our energetic state. The hardest part is getting better at noticing that it needs shifting. And the second-hardest part is convincing ourselves to just do the thing that will help move the energy. It can literally be a thirty-second activity. If we allow ourselves to get into it and embrace the moment, the results speak for themselves.

The reason we want to raise our vibration (notwithstanding our compassionate acceptance of all the vibes and the full spectrum of emotions) relates to the theory of the law of attraction.

The Law of Attraction

The law of attraction is the universal law that probably gets talked about most, at least in popular culture. It was the secret life hack that was at the centre of the popular book and film, *The Secret*. The law of attraction states that we will call in—or, attract—people, experiences and opportunities that match the vibration we are in. In other words, "like attracts like."

So if you are constantly in a negative, judgmental, fear-ridden place, you are going to attract more of those types of things into your life. If you are constantly fearing the worst outcome, well, guess what, those outcomes will probably happen more (or at least that's what you're more likely to see and notice). By contrast, you know how some people just seem lucky? According to the law of attraction, people who look for the positive in a situation, who believe that good things will eventually come to them (or that the negative things that are happening in their life are going to be for their ultimate good), those people will attract more uplifting, positive experiences and people into their life.

So, depending on what frequency you are vibrating at, those are the kind of things you are going to attract into your life. Like attracts like. Another common phrase that relates to the law of attraction is: "where focus goes, energy flows." In other words, if you focus on the negative, that's where your energy will flow, and you will call in more of the same. During my competitive fast-pitch softball days, one of my favourite coaches used to remind us: "Whether you think you *can*, or you think you *can't*—you're right." I think it's an old Henry Ford quote, but it's got staying power.

Manifestation

The law of attraction and vibrational energy are also tied in with the concept of manifestation. Manifestation is the process of bringing your desires, goals, and intentions into reality through focused thoughts, beliefs, and actions. At a more fundamental (and woo-woo) level, it's about aligning your inner world with your desired external reality.

It's a mindset practice that requires you to see, feel, and believe that the things you desire are truly destined for you.

I used to ascribe to the philosophy of "I'll believe it *when* I see it," but when I flip into manifestation mode, I have found that my lens becomes one of: "*If* I believe it, *then* I'll see it."

"Be, have, do" is another way the process is sometimes described. If you are living in a place of doubt, resistance, and skepticism, but reciting empty affirmations about the joy and abundance you want to call in, don't be surprised when your reality doesn't shift. If you can embody, or be, the feeling state that you want to create more of, then by vibrating at that frequency, you *will* attract more of the same—or so the theory goes. Sara Connell explains these concepts, and many more, in her book *The Science of Getting Rich for Women*. I highly recommend checking that one out.

One of the coolest things about manifesting is that you can use it for small day-to-day things, or huge life goals or shifts. For example, long before I was in the world of woo, one of the things that I randomly got into the habit of doing when I would drive into a busy parking lot was to say in my mind, "I'm so lucky with parking spots; I always get rockstar parking." And guess what . . . more often than not, I do!

CHAPTER EIGHT

MANTRA #8:

I always get rockstar parking! *

There are tons of manifestation tools and techniques out there. One such tool that, I confess, I used to silently mock is a vision board. I thought they were cheesy, and I doubted that cutting a bunch of pictures out of magazines and gluing them onto a poster board could change my life in any way. I have recently become a convert and have made vision boards for the last couple of years as a New Year's intention-setting kind of exercise. My vision board is, admittedly, hung in a lesser-trafficked part of my house so that not everyone who visits my home sees it. But it's in a spot where I see it often. On it, I've included images that are meaningful or symbolic for me. My current vision board has an owl on it, photos of some of my happy places—the forest, me travelling the world—as well as some words of things I want to remind myself to embody, such as "ease" and "celebrate." One of my divine-timing-related mantras is on there as well: "What is meant for me will not pass me by."

Celebrity mindset coach Laura St John is a treasure trove of ideas for manifestation exercises. One that she's famous for is called a "Flip It" list, a great tool for reframing the things in your life that you're not happy with, and flipping the focus from those negative thoughts to the positive version of that desire. Once you've figured

---

*NOTE TO SELF: Girl, it's time to aim higher . . .

Fig. 2. Secret (not so secret) vision board

out what you *do* want, instead of what you *don't* want in your life, the next step that Laura suggests is to write yourself a "Congratulations!" card from your future self (about six months into the future) to your current self, congratulating you on the positive changes that you're about to make.

On *FutureMe.com,* you can write and "mail" a letter to your future self as a manifesting exercise or practice. According to the site, they've delivered over twenty million letters in twenty years.

I know people who have used techniques like these to manifest new relationships, new clients for their business, their dream home, and even free gas! If you can dream it, you can manifest it, my friends. Indeed, some folks in the spiritual community say that you are only dreaming it *because* it's a real possibility for you; the Universe wouldn't show you those things unless they were truly available to you.

Energy Healing

Energy healing is a broad term that encompasses dozens of techniques from ancient forms of medicine, like Ayurveda and traditional Chinese medicine. Generally speaking, energy healing involves a practitioner channelling healing energy or working with a person's energy to restore balance and improve the health of the person's body and mind.

Whereas the Western medical model is primarily focused on curing and fixing, energy healing focuses more on the source than the symptom and works at a deeper level than the Western medicine practices most of us are used to. To be clear, I am not suggesting that energy healing techniques can or should be used to the exclusion of Western medicine . . . Both can be effective and both have their place!

Energy work is painless for the most part and does not come with many (if any) risks or side effects. Sort of the opposite of those pharmaceutical ads we've all seen on TV, where the people on the screen look like they are happy and thriving, meanwhile the narrator is talking at warp speed to let you know that "side effects of [the medication] could include—" a few dozen things that could happen to your body, ranging from the somewhat tolerable to the downright horrendous. But I digress.

Energy healing is centred around the notion that healing can take place by tapping into and utilizing the energetic field that courses through and surrounds each one of us. People use lots of different names to describe this energy force—many of which are discussed elsewhere in this book—including things like: life force, *qi* (aka *chi* or *ki*), aura, and *prana*.

Many energy healing modalities induce a state of deep calm and relaxation; I have experienced this personally from more than one type of treatment. This, of course, can be healing and restorative in and of itself. There's also a growing number of scientific studies speaking to the impact that energy healing can have on a person's physical and emotional health.

After a treatment, it is very common for people to feel more alert, clear, and grounded. It's like there's this veil of calmness enveloping your whole body that can last for hours or days.

Here's a quick rundown of some energy healing techniques that have come to my attention:

★ **Acupuncture/acupressure:** Spoiler alert: one involves punctures (but the needles are so very tiny, you barely feel anything) and the other involves pressure. Both are part of an ancient healing model based on balancing the chi as it flows through the body's meridian system.

I knew about acupuncture, but had never tried it until I was well into my concussion recovery. It almost felt like a "Hail Mary" because I was still desperately searching for answers and badly wanted to feel better, but I didn't think that acupuncture would help me. I tried it almost just to tick the box and say I had—turns out it was one of the best things I could have done. Based on a recommendation from a good friend, I was guided to an extremely talented and gentle acupuncturist named Delphine, who helped calm my nervous system, clear energy blockages, and perform all manner of other resets that I won't even pretend to understand the ins and outs of. Again, I have no idea why or how it worked; all I knew was that I felt better and better every time I left an acupuncture session. I am still an acupuncture devotee to this day.

★ **Reflexology:** It involves massaging or applying pressure to different parts of the foot, which are said to correspond to various body parts and organs. The right amount of pressure applied in just the right spot can relieve pain in your shoulders, for example, or help give your kidneys a boost. It's no secret that there are gajillions of nerve endings in the soles of your feet (well, about 200,00 in each foot, to be precise), so do yourself a favour and find a skilled reflexologist. It just might change your life. You'll walk out of the appointment in a blissful haze that normally takes six hours at the spa to achieve (I speak from experience . . . I don't think I'll ever drop reflexology from my arsenal of self-care and well-being modalities).

★ **Reiki:** This is one of the oldest and most widely practised forms of energy healing. At its core, Reiki involves a practitioner transferring universal energy through their hands into the client. Reiki can be practised in person (and may involve light touch), or it can be done virtually. This is one of those "if I hadn't experienced it first-hand, I wouldn't believe it" type things, but distance Reiki works—mind-blowing but true. Call it the placebo effect, if you will. I'm not expecting you to simply take my word for it, but I do stand behind what I've experienced.

★ **Craniosacral Therapy:** CST is an interesting crossover kind of modality. It's a gentle, hands-on alternative therapy that focuses on releasing tension in the craniosacral system (the membranes and fluid surrounding the brain and spinal cord). With light touch, the practitioner opens up cerebrospinal flow and attunes to the body's craniosacral rhythm. CST has been recognized in scientific studies, particularly in the osteopathic and dental-medical fields. However, its extremely subtle, almost hypnotic treatments mean there are still many who are skeptical about this therapy. Interestingly, some practitioners disavow any relationship between CST and the spiritual realm, while others acknowledge the connection upfront and suggest that therapists of this modality earnestly and intentionally seek to receive wisdom from the body they are treating in the form of physical, energetic, and spiritual awareness. I have tried craniosacral therapy, but it didn't resonate for me as much as some of the other energy healing modalities.

★ **Quantum Touch, Healing Touch, Therapeutic Touch:** These are therapies that typically involve placing one's hands lightly on (or very near to) the patient's body. Through the practitioner's use of light touch, breathing techniques and mindful meditation or grounding, they seek to influence the chi (or life force) of a person, which can then stimulate that person's self-healing capacities.

★ **Sound Healing:** This is a practice that uses sound frequencies to heal specific physical, emotional, and mental health issues. Sound healing sessions can involve the use of any number of instruments, including crystal bowls, Tibetan singing bowls, the didgeridoo, tuning forks, and even the human voice. The terms sound healing and **sound bath** are often used interchangeably, and this type of healing can be done either in a one-on-one session (where the patient is lying down and a practitioner is applying different sounds over various points in their body, including specific chakras), or in a group setting where immersive healing sounds are played, but individualized or targeted treatment is not usually done.

★ **Shamanic Healing:** This is a form of healing where a shaman draws in assistance and energy from the spiritual realm and invokes spirits, animal totems, or other spiritual helpers to assist them with healing. Practices can vary widely from one practitioner to another, but they typically involve vivid mental imagery and compassionate healing techniques.

CHAPTER NINE
EXISTENTIAL CRISIS

Sometimes it's tempting (very tempting) to think, "Okay, so if *everything* happens for a reason, and everything is *divinely timed*, then why is that person terminally ill? Why is that person in an abusive relationship? They don't deserve those things."

I get it.

And, no, they don't.

I think the trick here, for me, anyway, is not going the toxic-positivity route or trying to "grin and bear it" through an experience that is truly hard and truly shitty. Not at all. In my experience, the more authentic way to move through something yucky or hard is to acknowledge that what you're going through *is* hard, and it *does* suck, and then to try to remember to trust that there's a much larger plan at work. As impossible as it will be to see it at the time, these things are happening *for* us, not *to* us.

I was crushed when my marriage turned into an absolute dumpster fire after my daughter was born. *There were soooo many lessons there for me to learn. It would take a whole separate book to cover all of those.* But, having done a lot of inner work since that phase in my life, I now truly appreciate why all of those things had to happen and what the larger purpose was. Bonus: I got a beautiful daughter out of it who I would not trade the world for, and I'm at a place in life where I don't think I've ever felt more fulfilled or content. Clarity, man, it helps!

All of which is to say, whether you've met your spirit guides or not, and whether you're currently in a smooth patch or a rough patch, trust that they and the other members of your spirit team are around you, and they are working to help you make choices and take actions that are in service of your highest path. And yes, even when things are in the shit, they are there with you too. They won't interfere with your free will, so they let you make decisions and mistakes if you need to. And let's face it, we all need to make mistakes some of the time. Your guides will also try to help guide you—sometimes softly and gently, sometimes loudly and clearly—back towards your most aligned path.

◇◇

MANTRA #9:

Things are not happening to me.

They're happening for me.

◇◇

A Little Help Over Here

It took me a lot of introspection and time to wrap my head around everything that had happened in my life since my pursuit of health and my exploration of all things woo. What started with just meditation has since led me in so many new directions.

So far, my pursuit of learning has made a profound impact on my life, heart, health, and future. I wanted to follow those breadcrumbs as far as they'd take me, including the ones that led to my spirit guides.

I liked the idea that I have spirit guides looking out for me, and I wanted to learn as much as I could about them.

I learned that one of the best ways to communicate with your spirit guide (your whole spiritual team, really) is to invite them in. That means asking them for their assistance, their help.

Spirit guides are not pushy most of the time. They wait to be invited in. So it's super important for you to consciously invite them in, and to also thank them when you have received a message from them. Expressions of gratitude and acknowledgement of their involvement in your life are what keep the spirit guides coming back to help. If you are walking around thinking, "Damn spirit guides, why aren't they helping me more," or "Why wasn't my guide there when I needed them?"—well, you're quickly going to become the server's least favourite table in the restaurant, and you probably won't get as good service as the friendly, appreciative customer does.

My Spirit Animals

Luckily for me, you don't just get one spirit animal per lifetime (otherwise I'd still be feeling like the butt of a cosmic joke after the cougar card in that first visit to the metaphysical store). That being said, if I had only Googled "cougar spirit animal" at the time, I would have learned that the cougar as a spirit animal represents strength, wisdom, courage, and independence. Cougars are seen as powerful and solitary creatures, moving through the world silently and effectively. They are associated with power, freedom, and the ability to navigate difficult situations. Pretty badass if you ask me!

My spirit animals revealed themselves to me during the beach breathwork sessions in Mexico. *(Add this sentence to the top of the list of things this lawyer never, ever thought she would write—let alone publish—for all to see . . . but we're in too deep now, so I'll just keep going.)*

The animals who revealed themselves to me as spirit animals during those breath journeys were the lion (unexpected, but very welcome), as well as the snake and the phoenix (less surprising, but equally welcome). They showed up in ways that were not only symbolic and profound but also lighthearted and joyous.

More recently, I've started seeing images of owls everywhere. The theory is that if something is being placed in front of you and into your consciousness, it's for a reason—the Universe likely has a message for you or wants you to look into what it symbolizes. I realize now that I was seeing owls for a while before I took notice. When you aren't getting the hint or taking the lesson, Spirit tends to turn up the volume so that you can't help but notice.

A few weeks ago, I was out for a walk in a forested area near my home called Mystic Vale—yes, that's its real name. (You just can't write this stuff sometimes!) I was feeling disheartened and dejected after a misunderstanding with a close family member. I rounded a bend on the trail and saw an actual, real, live owl, standing on the path in front of me. I stopped mid-step and tried not to gasp in awe. It looked at me for a moment and then flew up into a tree nearby. I took a couple of pictures from the ground, in which the owl, of course, looked more like a giant blob of leaves or a nest in the trees than the actual owl it was.

Before I continued on my walk, I messaged a woo friend: "OMG!! I just saw an owl. It was on the path right in front of me, then it flew into a tree. Wonder what this means?!" I was still in awe. I had been walking this trail for years and never once had seen an owl before.

I left the vale and headed home. A few blocks from my house, I shit you not, there was a double rainbow in the sky! It felt like my spirit team and the Universe were shouting at me and had some important messages they wanted to convey to me that evening.

As you might have guessed by now, much excited googling and texting ensued as I delved into the symbolism behind what I'd just seen. The articles and posts that I read helped me make sense of what I was going through and were a comfort to me as I navigated the next few days.

Was this all just pure coincidence? Maybe. Could I be sure of that? Absolutely not. Instead, I chose (and will continue to choose) to look for meaning in the things that come into my life. I take solace and advice from the symbols that I feel Spirit is placing in front of me. Call it hogwash, call me naive, I'm not sure I care anymore because it feels better to me to believe that there's some order to the chaos instead of believing that it's all futile. I like that people (and sometimes animals) come into our lives for a certain reason, and at a particular time.

The Numbers Don't Lie

After the Costa Rica and Mexico retreats, life wanted to proceed as normal, as if everything was still normal. But *I* was not the same. I had evolved into a hybrid lawyer-woo version of myself.

Inside, I felt legally Zen. I knew that I could hold the whole truth (*and nothing but the truth*) of what and who I am. But externally, it felt impossible to embrace both sides of me at the same time. I still lived in two very distinct, separate worlds. In spiritual circles, I sometimes questioned whether I truly belonged. In legal circles, I feared that being open about my newfound spirituality would clash with the image of a sharp, no-nonsense lawyer who knew her stuff and demanded to be taken seriously.

Day to day, I was filled with excitement and anticipation around my explorations of something more. I wished I could shout it from the rooftops so everyone could experience what I was experiencing.

I wanted other people like me to understand the feeling of limitless potential that was now my norm.

I was out for after-work drinks one day with a friend of mine, named Toni. Toni is a business owner, and she leads a pretty mainstream life like me, so I was surprised when she laughed and said, "Hah—it's 5:55 pm. I keep seeing the number 555 everywhere! It's really weird."

"Maybe it's your angel number," I exclaimed, before I could stop myself.

Toni arched an eyebrow. "My what?"

For probably only the third or fourth time in my life, I shared my woo side with someone who had mostly just known me as Lawyer Kat.

"Different numbers have different meanings, and by showing you the same number over and over, your angels or spirit guides are trying to grab your attention and communicate with you. 555 must mean something." The words spilled out so easily, it shocked me. Where was the hesitancy? The fear of being insta-wrapped into the pin-striped straitjacket for lawyers who had gone off the deep end?

"Okay, so what does 555 mean?" Toni asked, sounding less than convinced.

"Let's Google it!" I pulled my phone out, and we looked up the meaning of the angel number.

From what we read, angel number 555 is a message that someone is in a preparatory state. The angels are trying to tell them to focus on their freedom as it pertains to their happiness and to embrace transitions that can make their lives better.

"It looks like angel number 555 is a sign from the Universe to let you know that you can welcome those transitions with open arms," I said.

Toni's eyes widened, and she was quiet for a moment as she picked at an invisible flaw on her perfect gel nails. In a partial whisper, she said, "A lot is going on in my life right now that I haven't shared with anyone yet . . . But all I can say is that this is bang on."

"Kat, do you really believe these coincidences are actually God or the Universe talking? I mean, coincidences happen all the time."

"I get it," I admitted. "I wonder all the time whether we're just looking for patterns and assigning meaning," I admitted. "But I don't know . . . Maybe both can be true? I think all of us are always looking to make meaning from the world around us. Our brains can't help but detect patterns and connections . . . It's part of our survival instinct or something, isn't it? So it's natural to look for, and find, these coincidences and patterns."

"Like seeing 555 everywhere," Toni said.

"Right. I think we choose what we want to see, to some extent. Call it confirmation bias, anchor bias, or whatever you want. And I think God or the Universe or Spirit is always placing little hints and opportunities all around us. Sometimes we're not in the right mindset to see them. Or, all we see are the negative coincidences and connections (like when we're having a bad week and it feels like the world is conspiring against us). I think there are little miracles all around us, if we are willing to notice them."

Toni was nodding, albeit slowly. "Okay, cool. I'm sort of with you, but I'm not sure the woo-woo stuff truly exists. I do, however, believe that my intuition exists, and that the subconscious aspect of my body probably knows what I need to do, more so than the intellectual or logical part of me does. So when we see these patterns, is it not just our intuition guiding us by highlighting patterns that our intellect will notice and pick up on?"

She made a good point. One that I had run through my mind many times. We debated and Googled a lot of woo that day, from angels, luck, and intuition to meditation and spirit teams. We even talked about the woo community's similarities to religious communities, of which there are many—gratitude practices are similar to giving thanks to God, all the angel stuff, the fact that there's often a charismatic, motivational style speaker on the stage, leading the way . . . It was great to talk about and share ideas, to put my tarot cards on the table, so to speak, for cross-examination. The lawyer in me was proud. The Woo Kat in me was even prouder.

A few months later, Toni divorced her spouse of twenty years. It turns out their relationship had been tanking. They had been trying to hang on for dear life, afraid of what a transition would look like and the impact it would have on their three kids.

555. The numbers don't lie.

Letting the Kat out of the Bag

After having spent the better part of the past four years moving through trauma and change and a lot of painful but necessary growth, I decided that I was ready to claim the upcoming year for myself. I declared that the coming year was going to be the Year of the Kat (notwithstanding that it was the Year of the Dragon on the Chinese zodiac).

This was also the year of my forty-third birthday. This might be a concept known only to elder millennials like me, but everyone has a particular birthday that is considered their "champagne" birthday. Your champagne birthday is when you turn the same age as the day of the month on which you were born. Sounds complicated, but it's not. My birthday, for example, is on the seventh of the month, which means my champagne birthday was when I was . . . seven years old. Not exactly Champagne-drinking age. So, I decided that when I turned forty-three (since $4 + 3 = 7$), I would make that my champagne birthday. Why the f not, I mean, I had already declared it the Year of the Kat and decided to have an ego-centric year, so why not go full out?

I decided that, in honour of my champagne birthday, I would throw myself a party. When you go out on a limb and throw yourself a party (including catering and live music), you invite everyone you know because you do *not* want it to be some lame-ass party where only three people show up. In my case, inviting everyone I knew meant inviting my lawyer and work friends, my spiritual friends, and my regular friends. Interestingly, in the Venn diagram of all of these groups, I was the only point of overlap.

Was I worried that my spiritual/retreat crew were going to out me to my law friends for doing the weird spiritual hippie shit that we do in the forest? *Yes.* Was I worried that these two different groups were going to look across the room at the other group, roll their eyes, and think "who are these weirdos?" *Most definitely.* Did any of that happen? *No!* We had the best time. I'm not sure what I was afraid of . . . It's not like some West Side Story rival gang confrontation was going to happen in my kitchen or anything. (Although I've gotta say, any party where there is an actual dance-off is pretty legendary, in my opinion.)

I'd been living separate lives—Lawyer Kat and Woo Kat—for so long, I guess I couldn't imagine the two different versions of me existing in the same space. One version kept me grounded, successful, and made it possible to have my daughter and put food on the table. The other version kept me believing in possibilities and, even more so, believing in myself.

Here's what *did* happen at the party. Everyone mixed and mingled, and people chatted and laughed. I heard friends exclaim to one another, "Oh! I've heard so much about you from Kat!" as they pieced together who they all were, and how they fit into the jigsaw mosaic of my life.

And when it was time for the live music to start, my friend Jennie, a talented singer-songwriter, took to the stage in the corner of my living room. She had asked me in advance for song requests, and I happily obliged because, although my singing voice leaves a little something to be desired, I've always been a huge music lover. A few songs into her set, Jennie paused to give a toast.

And then came the real tear-jerker moment; after her toast, she sang a song that she had written for me. It was called "Curious Kat," and it is, hands down, one of the sweetest things anyone has ever done for me. I'm not crying, you're crying. (Oh, who am I kidding, I'm bawling over here.)

I'd spent so much time worrying about keeping things secret and safe, looking strong, looking perfect, hitting my milestones, killing it at work, killing it at life—that I had been slowly killing myself. If my head hadn't hit the ground all those years ago, I might not have had the hundreds of different experiences and encounters that eventually led to that incredible moment on my forty-third birthday, spent with a collection of people I loved and who loved me.

As luck (and divine timing) would have it, I took the chance, leaned in, and didn't miss a thing.

CHAPTER TEN
Gen Zen

welcome

Let's be real: I had zero intention of falling into the world of woo, but I'm grateful I did. The more I venture into these uncharted waters, the better I understand myself, and the more whole I feel.

At times, it feels slightly illegal to feel this invigorated, alive, and at peace within myself. I realize this makes me sound like a certifiable nutbar who's inhaled too many incense fumes. But I can honestly say (under oath!) that woo has become my secret sauce for a life I am excited to wake up to each morning. I cringe when I think of how many opportunities I missed to better know myself and make peace with the parts of me I'd spent so long hating. Life is short, and I spent too much of it missing out on the chance to make these new, deep, meaningful connections with beautiful souls who were willing to see me for me—no judgment, no agenda, just kindness, openness, and understanding.

Over the past few years, I've met plenty of people just like me—mainstream folks who keep their woo-selves tucked away safely in the closet. What I have discovered among this cohort of people is an overwhelming sense that outing oneself as a spiritual person—or even a person who dabbles in spiritual practices—is risky.

I have lawyer friends who are reluctant to talk about the fact that they do breathwork journeys regularly and microdose psilocybin on weekends. I have met accountants, hairdressers, actors, bankers, business owners, and teachers who are similarly tentative about revealing their spiritual side, lest people judge them or not want to work with them in their respective professional contexts.

The Case for Woo

If I've learned one thing spending most of my adult life around professionals of all kinds, it's that we all love a good "business case." Well, here it is: spiritual practice could very well be the secret weapon that gives you the edge you've been missing. I wish everyone knew how good life could feel. But that's impossible unless I use my voice and share what I've experienced—hence why I've reluctantly decided to out myself by writing the book I didn't want to write.

MANTRA #10:

I am aligned. I am dialled in.

I am unfuckwithable.

〰️

Meditation and other spiritual practices can make you sharper, calmer, and more composed. They will help you feel dialled in. You will almost certainly feel more aligned, more confident in your decisions, and decidedly more "un-fuck-with-able." Not only have I experienced the huge amount of personal wealth and reward to be gained from doing this inner work, but, coincidentally, more and more scientific research and practices are now also backing it up.

From breathwork to mushrooms, science has joined the conversation:

- A systematic review of early interventions found that EMDR applied within three months of trauma significantly reduced PTSD symptoms at post-treatment and the three-month follow-up, though longer-term effects require more study. (*https://pubmed.ncbi.nlm.nih.gov/38626564/*).

- A December 2024 randomized trial involving frontline COVID-19 clinicians found psilocybin-assisted therapy led to a 21-point average reduction in depression scores, compared to a ~9.3-point reduction with placebo. (*https://www.axios.com/local/seattle/2024/12/05/study-magic-mushroom-therapy*)

- Additional trials funded in Canada are underway targeting psilocybin-assisted therapy for alcohol use disorder, treatment-resistant depression, and cancer-related distress, with multi-million-dollar funding in progress. (*https://www. canada.ca/en/institutes-health-research/news/2023/06/ psilocybin-assisted-psychotherapy-research-grant.html*)

- A March–April 2025 meta-analysis reported that transcendental meditation practitioners (ages 20–72) had lower expressions of pro-aging and inflammation genes, better cognitive scores, and healthier cortisol profiles. Older meditators performed cognitively on par with younger non-meditators. (*https://nypost.com/2025/04/16/health/ anti-aging-benefits-linked-to-one-surprising-health-habit/*)

- A Frontiers in Physiology review concluded that "deep breathing exercise (DBE)" can lower blood pressure by ~3–6 mmHg systolic and reduce stress, effects linked to improved autonomic balance and heart-rate variability. (*https://www. frontiersin.org/journals/physiology/articles/10.3389/ fphys.2023.1040091/full*)

- An earlier systematic review (2018, Frontiers in Human Neuroscience) detailed how 5–6 breaths per minute (coherent breathing) aligns heart and breath rhythms, producing measurable physiological benefits tied to stress reduction. (*https://www.nature.com/articles/s41598-023-49279-8*)

And while there are studies that measure decreases in blood pressure, lower cortisol, and less heart rate variability (HRV), the common denominator that we can't ignore is that results are largely based on how you feel—and thus are ultimately subjective: how you slept; whether you feel less, more, or the same amount of depression, stress, or anxiety; and how much pain you're in.

Yes, the lawyer in me tends to favour objectivity and evidence-based studies. But the human in me likes how, at the end of the day, the thing that matters most is all of this stuff makes us *feel*. If this is the placebo effect, then okay. I'll take this feeling however I can get it.

Joe Dispenza writes at length about the placebo effect, quantum physics, and epigenetics in his books, *Breaking the Habit of Being Yourself* and *You Are the Placebo*. Dispenza references one particular study in which participants were asked to do a strength training exercise with their finger against the resistance of a spring. The group who physically performed the exercise showed a thirty percent increase in muscle strength, while the group who only performed the exercise mentally—and never actually lifted a finger—had a twenty-two percent increase.

Out of Hiding

I have cautiously and slowly revealed aspects of my spiritual side to people around me, all the while holding my breath and bracing for ridicule. *How sad. Kat has lost her mind.*

Thankfully, I did not feel shunned by anyone I told, and instead, I felt *more* connected and *less* alone. Turns out there are WAY more people like me out here than I realized. But if we all keep doing this stuff in secret for fear of judgment, we are missing out on a huge opportunity to find and connect with more of our people.

I have discovered that there is an entire population of people who are into woo but are, like me (until now), living double lives, with one foot in the backyard yoga yurt and the other in the double-mortgaged, work-till-you-drop, normie world. On the surface, it looks like an Apple vs Android or Crips vs Bloods type of situation. But behind closed doors, it's a hands-over-heart, judgment-free zone, and everyone's invited.

I've decided that this group of people, for whom woo is no longer a bad word, deserves its own name. Some of them are mainstream professionals who look like me (suits, heels, briefcases), some live in Lululemon whenever possible (um, *also* me), and some wear long flowy clothes and hang dream catchers and crystals from their rear view mirrors (maybe soon-to-be me—not that there's anything wrong with that). More importantly, many of them choose work-life balance and view self-care as non-negotiable; they aren't afraid to look inward and make peace with the demons and shadows that haunt them; they aren't afraid to make deep connections with others and expect more from life . . . They've earned a name that's just for them, and as far as I'm concerned, "Gen Zen" fits all of these descriptions.

Gen Zen is made up of people who share a vague, hard-to-put-your-finger-on feeling that there *must* be something out there bigger than us. They sometimes identify as "spiritual but not religious" (not that the two are mutually exclusive), or they may just not have thought much about these things until now. I know I hardly gave any of this stuff a second thought while I was ramping up the speed on the treadmill of my adult life; I was too busy thinking about my billable hours, my next vacation, and the next trendy restaurant my friends and I were going to hit up. (And to be clear—there's nothing wrong with any of that, either.)

One of the best parts about Gen Zen is that there are no age limitations. We may not share specific decades like Gen Xers or Millennials, but we share other, more fundamental, traits—we have similar experiences, challenges, and vocabulary. We seek to understand ourselves and each other on a deeper level, and we view the world through a similar lens that looks well below the surface.

Membership into Gen Zen is automatic once you decide you want to explore inner growth and/or once you admit to yourself that you want to delve a little deeper and acknowledge that, surely, life isn't *just* about who wore what to the Met Ball or what mortgage rates have been doing lately.

Gen Zen represents this wonderful wooish community of people who aren't necessarily like-minded people as much as open-minded and open-hearted, bonded by a curiosity around spiritual practices, deep inner work, and living as authentic a life—a Zen life—as possible during our short time here on this planet.

In Gen Zen, the woo-curious are just as welcome as the woo-skeptical. And, most importantly, *you* are welcome, just as you are.

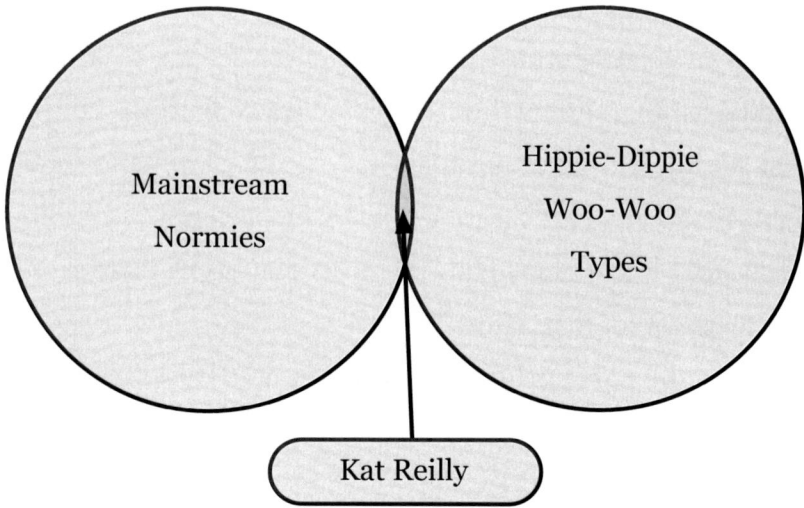

Fig. 3. How it used to feel

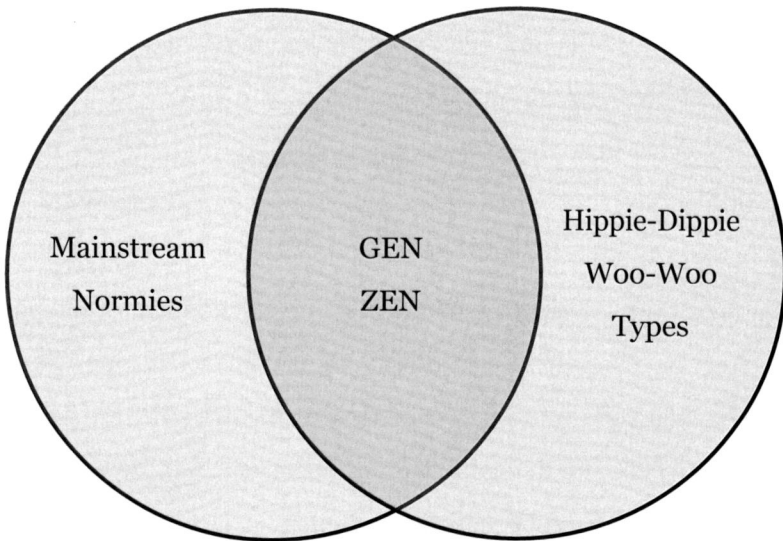

Fig. 4. How I've realized the world is

As Curious Kats do, I went down the research rabbit hole a few times along my spiritual journey, looking for answers.

In a study called "Spirituality Among Americans," Pew Research Center reported that seven in ten US adults describe themselves as spiritual in some way, including 22 percent who are spiritual but not religious." Want to join me in this rabbit hole? Check out the study. (*https://www.pewresearch.org/religion/2023/12/07/ spirituality-among-americans/*)

The study found that:

- 83 percent of all US adults believe people have a soul or spirit in addition to their physical body.
- 81 percent say there is something spiritual beyond the natural world, even if we cannot see it.
- 74 percent say there are some things that science cannot possibly explain.
- 45 percent say they have had a sudden feeling of connection with something from beyond this world.
- 38 percent say they have had a strong feeling that someone who has passed away was communicating with them from beyond this world.
- 30 percent say they have personally encountered a spirit or unseen spiritual force.
- Overall, 70 percent of US adults can be considered spiritual in some way because they think of themselves as spiritual people or say spirituality is very important in their lives.

That same study revealed that four in ten people meditate at least a few times a month, to either connect to their true self or with something bigger than themselves.

I've learned that spirituality can mean a lot of things to a lot of people. It can take many forms. It can be as simple as a guided meditation or a peaceful walk in nature, or it could take the form of receiving a download from Spirit or experiencing an ego death during an Ayahuasca journey. Either way, I'd bet my next lofty lawyer paycheque that the fundamental, underlying purpose is the same: people turn to spirituality to feel connected and to find what feels good.

How spiritual you are doesn't matter. What you feel and how you show up in the world does.

The Pew study showed that belief in spirits or the spiritual realm beyond this world is widespread and growing. And this, in turn, means that Gen Zen is so much bigger than anyone realizes (see Fig. 4).

Another thing I intuitively knew to be true, which was confirmed by the Pew study, is that folks who identify as spiritual are not immersing themselves in formal communities or congregations nearly as often as people who identify as religious.

This is another (huge) reason I felt compelled to write this book. We live in a world where digital connection is on the rise, and real-world, in-person connection is sadly lacking. And, at the same time, the percentage of people who identify as religious is declining, while those who consider themselves spiritual are rising by nearly the same proportion. In other words, it's pretty common to be spiritual or woo-curious and not be affiliated with any kind of formal spiritual or religious community. *Bottom line:* nowadays, it's easy to feel isolated, like we are the only ones asking these questions or doing this work, but in reality, there are tons of us with the same curiosities and interests. *Enter, Gen Zen:* A way for all of us doing similar work to connect and name our shared identity.

It may feel like we are all doing this stuff in our individual silos, but I'm here to let you know that's simply not true.

Spiritual Enough

Within a few years, I went from no woo to questioning whether I'm "spiritual enough" to be at a particular event or in a particular group. (Turns out, impostor syndrome can appear anytime, anywhere.) Now I know better. Am I spiritual enough to go to a breathwork retreat in Costa Rica? *Yes.* Am I spiritual enough to take my kid to swimming lessons one night and attend a sound healing ceremony the next night? *Yes.*

As I'm sure you can tell, I love my spiritual peeps, even when some of them are so steeped in the world of *om, aya,* and *shakti* that it can feel a little intimidating to the rest of us. Lingo gets thrown around that I found a bit off-putting at first. The first time someone asked me if I "received any downloads" during a group meditation session, I didn't know what to say. Then, they proceeded to tell me all about their many downloads as if it were something that I should already have been experiencing . . . I had no idea what downloads were and was too shy to ask. Then, there was the time someone wrote off something I said by replying, "That's just your programming talking." (That one felt like a bit of an affront.) Maybe it's just me, but I didn't and don't like being reduced to an empty vessel without a thought of my own until society, the government, or the normies program one into me. There's a lot more to my life and mind than that, thanks.

Don't let the woo/spiritual jargon deter you. Gen Zen is largely an inclusive space, and you are invited to come as you are and stay as long as you like. This is how you will find not just belonging, but true connection.

In *Daring Greatly*, Brené Brown wrote, "Connection is the energy that is created between people when they feel seen, heard, and valued; when they can give and receive without judgment. Belonging is the innate human desire to be part of something larger than us. Because this yearning is so primal, we often try to acquire it by fitting in and by seeking approval, which are not only hollow substitutes for belonging, but often barriers to it." She speaks and writes a lot about vulnerability being essential to better connection and belonging. "True belonging only happens when we present our authentic, imperfect selves to the world."

What could be more vulnerable than an emotional breakdown (and breakthrough) on the shores of a remote beach in Mexico, jumping off a waterfall into the arms of new forever-friends in the middle of the jungle, or writing this book?

My Gen Zen Meet-Cute

Every good movie or television show has that first dramatic meeting between main characters who are destined for love—their meet-cute.

My meet-cute with Gen Zen happened while half-naked in a hotel room on a business trip.

I was padding around the hotel room in my terry cloth, hotel-branded robe and decided I wanted to meditate outside that morning. I had been upgraded to a suite, so I had an outdoor deck to sit on. The city below was noisy, but the cool, fresh air felt good. Once I had my coffee in hand and my cozy socks on, I was good to go.

I sat cross-legged on the patio, thinking about some of the things I had recently been working on with my coach—my life's purpose and my life's work (*big frickin' topics!*). I was working on trusting my vision and thinking about the legacy I eventually want to leave behind. I dropped into meditation, and that's when the idea just landed in my head. Or my lap. Okay, both.

The words *Gen Zen* were spelled out across my field of vision, my consciousness. They were clear as day. My heart kicked into a new gear, and a rush of adrenaline swept through my body.

Gen Zen. It needs to be written down, a term that introduces other people like me to the spiritual concepts that I was once so hesitant to engage with, but that have helped me so much. A way for people to know that they're not alone in wanting to find "something more" in this life. More people need to know how useful this woo stuff is, even though they've probably written it off as a bunch of nonsense.

My marching instructions couldn't have been clearer.

The phrase Gen Zen was new, yet it was as if I'd heard those words a million times before and already knew and loved all that they represented. I am pretty sure that qualifies as a download of the highest order. In one moment, I was lost in thought, and in another, there was Gen Zen. It was the first time this had ever happened to me, but it was too strong to ignore. It was as if the words had their own temperature, weight, and colour. That's when I knew I had to write this book.

"Zen" is a word that I struggled with including. It's a word that has been overused in common parlance so often that it almost feels like it has lost its meaning. In some ways, Zen has become a synonym for chill or calm. But, at its root, it means more than that. I have read and researched and eventually cobbled together a definition of Zen that resonated with me, and encapsulates what I believe our generation is all about.

To me, Zen refers to a personal awakening, or a sense of enlightenment that can be achieved through meditation, intuition, simplicity, and self-contemplation, rather than blind faith. In other words, it involves looking inward instead of outward for truth, guidance, and wisdom. In this way, Zen is an inherently personal concept. It is custom-fit to each and every one of us.

This inward-looking focus is, for me, what distinguishes

spirituality from organized religion. Spirituality—at least in the way I practise it and the way those around me practise it—is not prescriptive. There are no hard and fast rules, no singularly authoritative texts, no commandments. (And no, I don't have any beef with any organized religion . . . in fact, I was raised loosely Christian and attended a United Church for part of my youth.) It's just that I have found that this flexible, customizable formula of practices is my preferred way of being. I like the Las Vegas-style buffet with all the spiritual flavours one could ever hope to taste.

Join the Club

When you first picked up this book, you probably fell into one of three camps: You wanted to find laughter and take delight in the story of a badass lawyer as she trades her law degree and grasp on reality for a Ouija board or satanic chant of some sort. Or, you were woo-curious and you wanted to learn along with me as I went on this exciting exploration of all things woo. Or, you were already a card-carrying member of Gen Zen (but you just didn't have a name for it until now), and were excited to read about a fellow member of the club. Either way, and no matter what camp you're in, thank you for being here. Truly—I'm grateful you're here.

◇◇◇

MANTRA #11:

You belong here. Come as you are. You are enough.

◇◇◇

Safe Starts

If you're inviting more woo into your life, I highly recommend starting slow. Please, please do not immediately sign up for an Ayahuasca journey, or a Vipassana (multi-day silent meditation) retreat. That would be considered jumping into the deep, deep end. Even if you're a daredevil who lives for the high diving board, some spiritual practices can be physically dangerous or potentially harmful to your mental and emotional well-being if they're not used with care—especially if you're not truly ready for it, or you're not being guided by someone with enough experience. (*You didn't think you were going to get through a whole book written by a lawyer without some kind of waiver or caution, did you?*)

In other words: go slow to go fast.

Who to Trust (and Who Not To)

I have been fortunate to have had nothing but amazing facilitators, guides, and coaches who have never led me astray in my exploration of woo. I can't imagine what it would be like if I didn't. I've heard some heartbreaking stories from friends and acquaintances who have been led on plant medicine journeys (Ayahuasca, psilocybin, etc) but have not had the proper guidance during the journey, much less the necessary integration after the medicine wore off. Instead of finding clarity and peace, they experienced trauma. Here are my best tips for safe starts and who to trust:

- Start with something easy to stop if it begins to feel out of control or uncomfortable. Guided meditations, oracle cards, crystals, and sound baths can all be lovely, gentle introductory options. In my opinion, it's not wise to start with plant medicine right off the hop, much less some huge spiritual journey involving travel to a far-off land with a facilitator you haven't worked with before.

- When something feels good, you want more. But my advice is to take it slow. There's no rush. Woo is a marathon, not a sprint. As tempting as it may be, doing all the things all at once and "stacking" your new spiritual practices isn't likely to serve you. You're much better off when you listen to your intuition, try out one or two practices you feel drawn to, and then let them integrate before moving on to the next shiny object, topic, or practice.

- Check out the facilitator's credentials and testimonials. In many ways, the spiritual world is a bit like the wild West. Some areas of it are credentialled, and some people will have certifications, but it's certainly not going to be the case across the board. Choosing facilitators because people you know and trust have worked with them and had positive experiences with them can be a good route to take.

- Respect your boundaries. Just because others are doing some kind of intense experience or medicinal journey doesn't mean it's right for you. True Gen Zen friends won't pressure you to try something if you're not feeling called to it. Listen to your gut, your inner knowing (your claircognizance). Practice getting quiet and listening to that voice inside, and find people who respect you when you use your Sacred No whenever needed.

Finding Your People

Let's be honest—making new friends and connections as an adult is hard for most of us. And let's just say that I was more than a little intimidated at times when I ventured into rooms I'd never been in before and tried out things I'd never tried before. Let me assure you that the people you meet in these rooms are, by and large, an open, accepting and very "you-do-you" crowd. Your Gen Zen spiritual peeps will be curious about what you're up to, but they won't be competitive. They will be rooting for your growth. They will hug you tight and sit right beside you when you are crying and healing, and they won't judge. If they do, they are not your people.

You can meet Gen Zen friends in real life (or IRL, as the kids say), of course, but online is great too. There's virtually no way you won't find people you connect with if you do a wee bit of looking around.

A friend I've known for over twenty years—who also happens to be a lawyer—said to me one day out of the blue, "Kat, I'm not sure what you're doing these days, but whatever it is, it's working. You seem so much happier and more at peace than I've seen you in a long time."

That hit me in the best way. Plus, it gave me the perfect opening to share a bit more with him about the inner work I've been doing. Just enough to spark a bit of curiosity. He later told me he had picked up a copy of Eckhart Tolle's *The Power of Now*.

Turns out, a dash of woo with a side of real-world results goes a long way.

EPILOGUE
FREEDOM

I got my laptop and case books set up at the counsel table and glanced up to where the judges would be sitting in a few short minutes. In the Court of Appeal, a panel of three judges hears your case. That's right, three of the smartest, most intimidating legal brains in the jurisdiction would momentarily be grilling me about the intricacies of my case, trying to poke holes in my arguments and see if my legal theory held up. It's high-pressure, high-intensity, and—when it goes well—downright exhilarating!

As I looked up toward the bench, I wondered if I would ever occupy one of those chairs. People had begun to ask me whether I had any interest in being a judge. I had been practising law for long enough (over fifteen years at this point), and I guess Operation Reputation had worked, because people in the legal community seemed to think that I had a shot at being appointed a judge one day.

These were questions that I did not have time to ponder, being that the hearing was about to start.

It was a hot bench that day (meaning I got a *lot* of questions from the panel). I was under fire, and so was my opposing counsel. After I completed my submissions (arguments, evidence, case law) and sat down, I felt pretty scorched. The questions had been tough. These judges were not convinced of the strength of my case, and their skepticism came through loud and clear.

Even so, they did not render a decision from the bench that day. Instead, they "reserved judgment." That meant they would consider the case over the coming days and weeks, and render a judgment after they had re-read the legal arguments and thought some more about the oral submissions made in the courtroom.

I left the courthouse that day exhausted, but satisfied. I had put my best foot forward and "left it all on the field," as they say. The rest was up to them.

There's something freeing about walking out of court knowing you've done all you possibly can and accepting that the rest is out of your control. It's not easy to just *let it go*, but I'm getting better at it. Worrying about the outcome at that point simply doesn't do you any good. You may as well take your team for cocktails and celebrate a job well done. Which is exactly what I did.

After a few dirty martinis, I went back to my office and put away my court robes and files. Then, I grabbed my luggage, ordered an Uber, and went to the airport.

That night, unbeknownst to my colleagues and most of my friends, I was going to be flying halfway around the world to visit my love interest—a man named Freedom, if you can believe it—who was currently travelling in India. Freedom and I met at a breathwork retreat and had become extremely close, extremely quickly. Freedom was much deeper into his spiritual journey than I was, hence his desire to immerse himself in the culture and teachings that India had to offer.

We'd been talking on the phone and by Zoom pretty regularly. Many of our talks were deep and vulnerable. And others were just lighthearted and silly. We connected in a way that I had never connected with anyone. But he was so . . . different from me. He was fully engaged in the world of spiritualism and woo. He was travelling around India like a nomad, meeting with spiritual gurus and learning new teachings. He was in *deep*. Way deeper than anyone else I knew. I was intrigued by him, but also wary of how different our lives looked. What was the point in even pursuing something?

Like the judges who heard my case that day, I was skeptical about what I was about to embark upon, but I decided I would reserve judgment. Keeping an open mind had served me well thus far. There was no denying that I was evolving into a happier, more balanced version of myself because of my new woo practices and exploration of spirituality.

Evidently, based on the flight ticket in my hand, I had also become more spontaneous. The old Kat would never have taken a week off work to fly fourteen hours halfway around the world to see a man whom, up to that point, I'd only spent a few days with.

Who was this person, and what had she done with the old Kat?

Following my heart instead of my head was not on brand. Logic and reason may be my bread and butter, but I've come to realize that they can only get me so far. So, I shelved (at least for a while) my litany of safe, reliable reasons to maintain the status quo and decided to jump. I jumped onto the plane, into the unknown, and toward a connection with someone who might (or might not) become very special in my life.

There was a magnet pulling me towards India, towards Freedom, and I was so incredibly curious as to what I would find there.

Acknowledgements

To my Mom, my sister, and my daughter: The women in my life are all important to me, but you are the three most important. Thank you for always being there. I love you.

To Jenn: You are the dream editor. I could not have asked for a better person to work with on this. You made this book a hundred million times better than it would have been. Thank you for writing with me, laughing with me, and crying with me.

To Sharleen and Crystal: Without the two of you, I'm not sure I would ever have started this book. I owe you a huge debt of gratitude.

To Jennie, Dave, Linette, Tyler, Aisling, and Chris: You saw this book in its raw form, and your feedback has been invaluable. I am forever grateful.

To the friends who have been with me since the beginning: Dixie, Rachel, Nathaniel, Kwang, Ingrid, Louisa, Meg, Hailey, and Josée. Thank you for your steadfast friendship as I explored and evolved.

Thank you to Spirit. The Universe. My Angels. Thank you for helping me learn to trust.

Last, but definitely not least, to my spiritual fam (Kyla, Ocian, Wesley, Cam, Ryan, Freedom, Mandy, Allison, Rachel, Samenda, Melissa, Dean, Lisa, Emily, Sabrina, Nicole, Natasha, Jacky and SO many others). I love you all. Thank you for being on this journey with me.

About the Author

Photo by Lea Vanderburg, Lea May Photography

Katherine "Kat" Reilly was born and raised in British Columbia, Canada. After spending some time during her early adulthood exploring different parts of the country and the world, she returned to the West Coast and has been a practising lawyer there for nearly 20 years.

At work, Kat is a relentless advocate, a skilled negotiator, and hates to lose. At home, Kat is a devoted mom to her beautiful, spirited 5-year-old daughter. When not working or parenting, Kat can often be found out in nature, sitting on her back deck with her journal and a strong coffee, or planning her next travel adventure.

Kat realized long ago that she was not like other lawyers. She is a deeply feeling empath and has, for the last several years, been on a quiet quest for something "more."

To find out more about Kat (or to download her favourite meditation mantras), visit *www.legallyzen.ca.*